What Price Freedom?

What Price Freedom?

PEGGY BROOKE

Ronald N. Haynes Publishers, Inc.

Palm Springs, California

WHAT PRICE FREEDOM?

 Ronald N. Haynes Publishers, Inc.

PALM SPRINGS, CALIFORNIA 92263-2748

Library of Congress Catalog Card Number 82-081139
ISBN 0-88021-073-7

This is a true story. Characters and incidents are authentic, although some of the names have been changed.

Scripture references are from the *New International Version*, Copyright 1978, by Zondervan Publishing House, and are reprinted by permission.

Excerpts from the article "My Baby Is Blind" by Peggy Brooke are reprinted by permission of *Today's Christian Woman*, Copyright 1981, by Fleming H. Revell, Old Tappan, New Jersey 07675.

Excerpts from the article "Frontier Challenge" by Peggy Brooke are reprinted by permission of *Guideposts Magazine*, Copyright 1981 by Guideposts Associates, Carmell, New York 10512.

Printed in the United States of America

Dedicated to
John,
whose courage and love have
shaped my life
and my story,

and to
Mom and Dad,
who always believed
I could reach any goal
I set my sights on.

With grateful acknowledgment to
Elaine Wright Colvin,
for editing, typing,
and offering
priceless advice and encouragement,

and to
Lenore Puhek
and
Cynthia Kenney,
for generously giving
their typing skills.

Table of Contents

Chapter 1

Swept off My Steed

John was a man of strong courage and faith. I was in love with him, yet we were as different from each other as ice is from steam. But young love, blind as it was, did not see that I admired in him what I lacked in myself. My courage could have been stored on the head of a pin and my faith would have fallen, like dominoes, at the touch of a finger.

I never guessed that love and marriage would demand that our differences merge. And I never dreamed how much the change would hurt.

It was 1967.

I met John, the president of our sophomore "Class of '70," in the cafeteria of Carroll College. Actually, that's where he met me. Although I had voted for his opponent because my roommate was his campaign manager, I knew John. How could I have missed him?

His friendly grin, touseled blond hair, and steady blue eyes held my gaze as I set my tray down across the table from him.

The waitress had directed my two girl friends and me

to the table where John and two other fellows were eating. How fortunate, I thought.

I smiled at John. Without thinking, I reached up to pat my shoulder-length brown hair.

My roommate, Suzy, the aggressive one, said, "Hi, John," through a wad of bubble gum. She pushed her glasses up on her pert little nose.

"Hi, Suzy," he replied evenly, a little smile playing across his tanned face. "Who are you campaigning for today?"

"Aw . . . no hard feelings, huh?" she bantered.

He glanced at me again and then introduced his friends.

"This is Pete Hilger and Brad Dolan . . . "

"Oh!" Suzy jumped. "Meet Peggy Murphy and Melissa Sundby," she gestured offhandedly at us and turned her attention to her mashed potatoes.

"Where are you from?" John's eyes met mine.

"North Da . . . "

"Hey, John, tell us where you're from," Suzy challenged. There was a glint in her eye. "Tell us about . . . Pony, isn't it?"

Melissa giggled.

John blushed. "I'm from Pony, Montana," he confided to me. "I bet you never heard of it."

I shook my head. "No."

I knew I was staring at him more than I should.

"Come on, John," Brad nudged him. "Sue wants to know what people find to do in Pony, Montana."

Pete leaned over to say something to me, and I joined in the teasing. Soon we were all laughing and poking fun at one another.

That night John called and asked me to go with him to the homecoming dance the next weekend. It was almost too good to be true.

I had come to the college town of Helena, Montana, from my home on a small farm in North Dakota. I loved the mountains around the Helena Valley. I loved Helena. And from our first date, I loved John.

"My dad owns a cattle ranch," he told me modestly the night of the dance. A year later he added, "And I loved only my dog and my horses—until I met you."

He left the ranch and studied accounting because ... well, because his older brother went to college. When he met me, he knew he'd chosen the right school.

I had been raised in the country, too. But, having grown up with four sisters and one baby brother, I never was interested in the outdoor activities of the farm. Once when desperate for excitement, I had ridden a cow, but I'd never even sat on the back of a horse.

John thought my inexperience a scandal. He borrowed some horses from a local rancher and, the next Saturday, took me out riding. I was too ignorant to worry about danger. I only hoped I would impress John that I was a fast learner.

The morning was bright, with just a nip of fall in the air. The meadow grasses waved, sparkling with dew. I was disappointed when I saw that John had brought his friend, Dan.

"He kind of invited himself along," John whispered as we climbed over the pasture fence. It made it all right, knowing John was disappointed, too.

John and Dan chose what looked like respectable mounts. I would describe my horse as being an old nag.

John knew I wasn't ready for anything spirited.

John gallantly made a step for my foot with his cupped hands and boosted me into the saddle. I caught my breath. I hadn't realized horses were so high off the ground! I hoped the thing steered well.

I forced my left hand to rest on my thigh. It yearned to cling to the safety of the saddle horn. I imitated the casual way John and Dan cradled the reins in one hand. This might be easy if everybody just keeps moving slowly, I thought. I tried to concentrate on the loveliness of the tree-shrouded mountains that encircled us. The farther ones were silhouetted in smoky green against the soft blue sky.

Our horses walked along together for awhile.

"You hold yourself really well in the saddle," John complimented me. His blue eyes shone.

I was glad he didn't guess my spine was bolt upright on account of every nerve being stretched taut with apprehension. Even at a walk my back was jolted badly. At a trot I was sure I'd get whiplashed.

The men's horses were pulling at their reins.

"Listen, guys," I suggested, "You go on ahead. Do some running or something. I know this is boring—going slow with me."

"Come on, John." Dan was ready.

"Oh, no, really. This is fine," John assured me. "You'll be able to keep up with us. Let's just ease into a trot."

"Oh, no!" I choked. "I mean . . . um . . . I mean I want to get more of a feel for the horse. Please go ahead. This mare is gentle . . . perfectly safe. I'm handling her fine." I laughed and tossed my hair confidently.

"Please," I touched John's hand as he still hesitated, "Please, go on and run the horses with Dan. You can come back and check on me in a minute," I added, seeing he was wavering. "I'll just be plodding along. I love the scenery." I gestured away from myself to the mountains.

Dan was off and John followed after another second's pause. He eyed my horse in that second as if reassuring himself that no one with a brain could have serious trouble making her obey.

John and Dan raced on ahead, their bodies seeming to roll with the movement of their horses.

They had been out of sight for a few minutes before I dared do a little experimenting. I urged the horse into a spine-splitting trot. Not too bad, I thought, if I manage to stay in the saddle.

I pulled on the reins and the horse slowed, almost throwing me off balance. I breathed easier. Thank heavens the horse had no ideas of her own!

I might as well keep practicing. I encouraged my horse to go even faster. I loved the feel of the wind blowing my thick hair.

Oops! The horse lunged, and I grabbed the saddle horn with my free hand. Suddenly the saddle lurched a bit to the right.

I'd listened to enough horse talk to know that I was in trouble. The cinch was loose. Fortunately the horse bounced to a stop when I yanked on the reins. The saddle slipped sideways in a gentle little arc that dumped me, not too unkindly, in a heap on the grass. The startled mare jumped sideways and galloped after the other horses, her ears perked, the saddle flapping under her belly.

I felt disgraced, a sure failure—not even able to stay astride a saddle for an hour. What would John—the rancher—think of me when my riderless horse caught up to him?

When John and Dan saw her, they thundered back—looking for me.

Worry was written all over John's face. "Are you all right?" he called, swinging a long leg over the saddle as his horse lurched to a stop.

"I'm fine!" I said as I straightened myself up, laughing nervously.

"You could have been dragged," he said seriously. He swept off his broad-brimmed hat and rubbed a hand through his unruly hair. "That cinch being loose had to be my fault. I thought I had it tight, but it's hard to tell on a horse as fat as she is. I should have checked her again."

"It's okay. Really." John's obvious embarrassment relieved me of mine. "The horse just stopped and I sort of slid off. I'm fine!" I felt foolish. He had the responsibility of worrying about cinches and all I'd worried about was looking good.

John grinned boyishly, his eyes twinkling. "You reacted fast and it kept you from being hurt."

I squeezed his hand. I knew then he wasn't looking for an expert horsewoman after all! On the contrary, John seemed to find my lack of horsemanship sweetly mystifying. His patience proved infinite, as this was the first of many riding sessions, none of which changed me into anything but a timid horsewoman, at best.

We were married in 1970 and spent our first "honeymoon" summer working on a dude ranch. John wrangled dudes—that is, he guided vacationers on horseback rides over mountain trails. I waited on tables in the log dining room. But even with hours of riding at the ranch, I remained a greenhorn, never quite overcoming my fear of horses.

In the fall we returned to Helena. I taught school while John finished his last year of college. After graduation, John landed a job as a bank accountant.

At the end of his first day at the office, he skipped upstairs into our furnished one-bedroom apartment and casually threw his sports coat across the back of a chair. He pulled a pencil from behind his ear and dialed the phone with the eraser end. We both dissolved in giggles as he strutted around the room flicking an imaginary cigar.

We celebrated! College lay behind us; two impressive careers—accounting and teaching—lay, like a superhighway, in front of us as far as we could see. We were set. And secure. We were on our way, at last, to the only kind of success we thought life had to offer.

"Peggy," John announced, taking me into his arms, "tonight is the first night you'll sleep with a young executive."

Chapter 2

Questions Dr. Spock Missed

"Rock. Rock, John." I said the words clearly so he would not miss my signal.

He glanced at me and then at his watch.

"Well, how many minutes?" I whispered, slipping across the grass to his side. My labor pains had started while we were entertaining guests, and we were trying to keep the news of the baby's imminent arrival to ourselves.

"Still seven," he whispered back. Then, as if protecting me from myself, he said, "Do you have to be so obvious?"

It was 1972; this was my first pregnancy. We'd been eating when I felt my first contractions. After dinner someone had suggested we all go for a hike up the hill behind our little trailer house.

To keep our secret but still allow John to time the contractions, John suggested I say "rock" in a sentence every time I had a pain. I was failing miserably at this game, giggling for no reason, oblivious to the conversation around me. The baby was finally coming! How could I keep it a secret?

Our son, Justin, was born at 4:59 the next morning. After staying a day and a half in the hospital, I bounced home, eager to "mother." But I soon discovered that I knew nothing about caring for a baby, and the endless hours I spent meeting his needs exhausted me. The sobering responsibilities of parenthood descended upon me and overshadowed my every breath for some time.

How lonely I felt for the quiet of John's undivided attention. I needed to pour out my uncertainty and exhaustion on his sympathetic ear. But there never seemed to be enough time. John was pushing himself hard. He'd taken a second part-time job on weekends to help fill in the gap made by the termination of my salary. We both agreed that my job description should change from teaching a classful to caring for and teaching our son.

When he was five days old, Justin developed a stuffy nose. I called the doctor, who gently assured me, the nervous mother, that nothing was wrong.

But the next day Justin's congestion worsened. By late afternoon he was struggling for every breath he drew through his tiny nostrils. Frightened, I called the doctor again.

"The baby may be allergic to your milk," he said. "Stop nursing him and begin feeding him formula."

I called my dear friend Melissa who rushed over, delivering a starter kit of Playtex bottles. She became the teacher. We sterilized the nipples and other equipment. We mixed the formula. How complicated it all seemed— or was my brain just numb from nervous exhaustion?

To stop the flow of milk, John bound up my swollen breasts with a dishtowel. He pulled the "corset" tight as he could and then tied a knot at the back.

That night, John fell soundly asleep, but I stayed awake, crying. My breasts throbbed with pain, but worse than that, I was terrified to fall asleep. I must listen for every breath of my baby. Would he stop breathing before morning?

The light of dawn found Baby Justin's nose completely plugged. He couldn't eat, as the sucking action of his lips and tongue against the bottle's nipple cut off the air supply through his mouth. Even John became alarmed. This time he called the doctor.

"I'm sorry, Mr. Brooke," John heard, "there is nothing I can do."

"Well, shouldn't the baby be in the hospital?" John demanded. "Shouldn't somebody see him? The little guy can't breathe!"

"All right. Meet me at the hospital." The doctor seemed resigned to placating our rookie parental fears.

At the hospital, nurses placed Justin in a clear plastic oxygen tent. A culture showed he had a staph infection.

For three days I sat beside his hospital crib almost continuously. What a relief having the hospital staff take charge of the baby. Still I could not relax. I knew I ought to slip home, into my bed, for a much needed nap; but I felt I had to prove myself a good, devoted mother. I stayed to watch over my baby.

I avoided looking at myself in the full-length mirror across from Justin's crib. My once-trim figure bulged revoltingly at the tummy. Even with a loose overblouse the dishtowel binding my chest gave me a boyish profile. I wondered what people imagined as the cause of the strange lump on my spine—the knot of the dishtowel. My eyes were puffy from lack of sleep and dark semi-circles filled the hollows below them. Even my thick brown hair hung limp and looked dull. I wanted no reminders of my present physical condition.

When we took the baby home again, the responsibilities of motherhood loomed over me, looking even larger and more frightening than before. My instinctive protectiveness grew into a mania of fear that Justin would become ill again. I mentally recorded every move the baby made; I never trusted him to anyone else's care. I hovered over him, making sure he ate precisely the amount of food recommended by the baby books—at precisely the right intervals.

Baby Justin was five months old before we visited my parents at their comfortable old North Dakota farm home. By observing my mother, I finally learned how to enjoy my baby. She was at such ease with him. As if the baby and I were both robots, I had followed every word of the advice given in baby care books. I had grown nervous when he had not responded exactly as the experts said he would. What relief my mother brought me. I could relax—even between Justin's naps. I learned to listen to Justin's responses—his protests when I pushed too much food at him, his need to skip his perfectly scheduled nap when he just wasn't tired. Both he and I were much happier than when I insisted on conforming to "the book."

When Baby Justin was nine months old, John and I bought our first house. Built in the Thirties, it was brick with shining hardwood floors and large, sunny windows.

The house proved to be good medicine for me. I had become bored with cleaning our tiny trailer and caring for my child. The new house filled my days with new challenges. I stripped old paint off the woodwork and repainted and wallpapered the plaster walls. I sewed lacy priscilla curtains for the wide dining and living room windows. John built kitchen cabinets and installed a double stainless steel kitchen sink where the old white enamel one had hung from the wall.

That spring lilacs peeked through my gingham kitchen curtains and white-blossomed mountain ash trees enclosed the little back yard. Just glancing out my pantry window at our one tall pine tree made me feel I was snuggled away in some private mountain cabin.

At last, everything in my world seemed perfectly in place. My husband had a good job, steadily moving up the banking ladder. We lived on a comfortable budget, even stashing a healthy amount into savings every month. Of course the future posed no problems. The bank provided generous insurance and retirement plans.

Housework was a joy; in fact, I grew a little meticulous in keeping things clean and in place, because I saw my home as so beautiful when all was in order. In a way, my home became a reflection of myself—a point of pride. I nearly saw my home and myself as one. My daydreams centered around making the house lovelier; and then my dreams flew further into the future—to the day we would sell it. What kind of profit would we make? How far up the materialistic scale would our next home be?

John's dreams were different from mine. He had begun to dislike his accounting job. He longed to escape the monotony of building and dismantling columns of numbers. He wanted to fly to the freedom of the out-of-doors.

John heard of a logger who would be hiring several timber fallers later that summer. This could be the opening he had been hoping for! He started making plans for his great escape. First, he bought an old four-wheel drive jeep in which he would drive to the mountains. With a little work, he said, it would be in running condition.

Every evening and all weekend for weeks he was in the driveway visible only from the waist down. His head and shoulders were buried under the hood of the old jeep or spread-eagled under the chassis.

It was early July when a roar and a cloud of black smoke announced the engine's start.

"Come try it out, Peggy!" John yelled through the screened back door. I left Justin napping to join him.

The jeep had long before lost its hood. It had gotten in John's way. The little green jeep stood shuddering and rattling as its motor reverberated in the driveway. I took my seat on the passenger side, finding a place for my tennis-shoed feet among the oily rags on the floor.

John beamed. His teeth flashed white, his eyes sparkled, like blue lake water, in his grime-streaked face.

He shifted into reverse and we lurched out to the street. Neighbors left idling lawn mowers, peeked around leafy caragana hedges, then strolled, grinning, out to the sidewalk. Children scrambled up on their father's shoulders to point and cheer us on.

I waved back. John and I held hands on the torn seat as the jeep bounced and shuddered down the street. Forgotten screwdrivers and wrenches jolted off the front fenders. A trail of tools and blue black smoke dropped behind us on the street. It was a glorious moment of triumph for the mechanically inclined; a day of hope for the office-bound dreamer.

But that afternoon, at the car wash, John hosed the jeep down—and the old engine died. "A cracked block," his autopsy revealed. It never ran again.

John continued working at the office. But he had found a new love; tinkering with machines. His dream, someday to leave the office behind, became unsquelchable. I continued my happy housewifery, not really conscious of what John's restlessness might eventually mean.

Chapter 3

Search for Something More

Those were the years of our spiritual unrest. Both John and I had been raised in traditional Catholic families. We faithfully attended Sunday mass, but it seemed Christianity promised more than we were getting. Something was missing.

One morning, after a typically boring Sunday service, John drove Baby Justin and me out to the mountains. He parked the car in a meadow on Mount Ascension, overlooking the Helena Valley.

The pungent smell of pine and the trill of meadowlarks greeted us. Below, warm sunlight glistened on rooftops and highlighted the dark and light greens of the trees lining the streets.

"The world is so peaceful and lovely," I murmured, leaning my head on John's shoulder. "What does the God who made all of this have to do with boring sermons and tired-out hymns?"

"I don't know. Maybe Frank is on to something,"

John mused. Frank was a neighbor who stopped by several evenings a week to talk to John about our need to be "saved" by making some sort of public declaration of Jesus as a "personal" Savior. I didn't trust Frank.

Still, I longed for something to fill my spiritual void.

I sighed and then admitted one of my gnawing worries: "How can we pass on any faith to Justin? We can't fake a faith we don't have, especially when Justin gets old enough to have doubts of his own."

We fruitlessly talked about our spiritual frustrations until, at last, John reluctantly drove back down the mountain.

Still we searched. I read a book that prophesied a coming stock market disaster. It urged everyone to prepare for the catastrophe.

Not wanting to be caught off guard, John and I loaded our basement storeroom with cases of extra food. We invested in four bars of silver bullion. (The book said this would be the only acceptable currency when our government collapsed.) Late one night John buried the bars in the dog pen in the back yard.

But still we didn't feel secure. On the contrary, I began to wonder how the grocery clerk would make change when we plunked a bar of silver worth four hundred dollars down on the counter to pay for a loaf of bread. And what if the neighbors were starving? How could we hoard our supply of food then?

Our survival plan didn't seem to be the answer to our fear of the future.

Eventually we used up our extra food. Because the price had fallen, we kept the silver for several years. Then, when the market rose again, the dealer who had sold it to us had lost interest in buying it back. He must have given up watching for the disaster, too.

We tried a new tactic for finding security. John and I invited our parish priest over. What answers could he give us?

At his suggestion, we joined a Bible study group he had formed. The first assignment was to read Matthew 14:22–33, the account of Peter and Jesus walking on the water. We would discuss it at the next class.

I read the familiar Scripture story, but with my usual frustration, even anger. Here was a perfect illustration of why I had so much trouble with faith. Jesus was always expecting intelligent, rational men and women to believe in unreasonable, outlandish things. Walking on water? It was impossible. If only the things He did and asked of us made sense!

But as much as I scoffed, I could not deny that way down inside of me I did believe. For some reason (was it my childhood training?), I believed the impossible—that Jesus of Nazareth had walked on the Sea of Galilee.

Then, like the warmth of the sun breaking through the clouds, the truth shone into my mind—faith was higher than intellect!

I couldn't reason my way to Jesus. Living by faith was on a higher realm than living by reason!

A few days later our neighbor, Frank, sent his pastor to our home. The pastor explained Romans 10:9 to us: "If you confess with your mouth, 'Jesus is Lord,' and believe in your heart that God raised him from the dead, you will be saved." The Bible proclaimed that faith in Jesus was all that was necessary to get to heaven! What a wonderful promise on which to base one's life.

Frank had given us a *Living New Testament*. I devoured it from cover to cover. I didn't know what was happening to me, but suddenly this Jesus whom I'd vaguely loved and tried to follow all my life was beginning to seem alive—and very real.

Someone at our Bible study told John about a weekly prayer meeting. We decided to try it out, and there met the strangest group of people. They had a noisy, abandoned way of praying that, at first, made me want to run away from them.

But I kept going to the prayer meetings; I wanted to hear more about their new kind of faith. They talked about Jesus as if they knew Him as an intimate and caring friend. They expected Him to take a personal interest in them. And they saw results that made a difference in their lives. They seemed to know what other people only hoped—that God loved them immeasurably.

After three or four prayer meetings, John and I agreed to put our trust as totally as we could in Jesus. We asked Him, in prayer, to take over every aspect of our lives. We promised, for our part, to follow Him faithfully.

The step of faith gave new hope to our lives! Sunday mass became a worship service in which we eagerly participated. It was a love-feast between ourselves and our great, persistent Lover. The little group of "strange" people at the prayer meetings soon became some of our closest friends. They shared our new vision of life—a vision that saw this world as only a shadow of the real world to come. Our lives took on meaning; we were preparing for that future land.

Our restless spiritual searching seemed finished, our void filled. But our life did not grow stagnant.

One night after John and I were in bed, we heard a faint sound, as if someone were tapping on a car horn.

"Funny," John whispered, "that sounds like the horn on the Falcon." The Falcon was our "second car." We had bought it for fifty dollars, when John and I had both been working. John had since cut off the back half of the roof and sides of the car and put a plywood wall behind the front seat. We called this car-converted-to-pickup-truck our El-Fal-Camino.

I followed John as he stole out of bed and crept to the dining room window, which overlooked the driveway. A faint light lit up the cab of the El-Fal-Camino. A pair of legs stuck out from under the open door.

"Someone's trying to 'hot-wire' it!" John exclaimed in a loud whisper.

The horn tooted faintly again, as if the fellow had clumsily bumped it with an elbow.

"He must be drunk!" John muttered, on the way to the phone. He couldn't see to dial the numbers until I found and lit a match.

The police came quickly and quietly escorted our bumbling burglar away to jail. The police officers knew the chronic drinker and overnight cell-warmer on a first-name basis.

Although the incident was almost laughable, it alarmed us. Was our neighborhood safe? We had owned our home for almost a year. We had noticed more and more strange activity in the apartment house near by. Because of the large assortment of strangers coming and going each day, we suspected someone inside of selling drugs. We read in the paper of a murder/suicide at that address. We had to decide: Was this where we wanted to raise our family?

Sadly, we put our house up for sale. We started looking for something more suitable. Almost immediately we
found a house on the outskirts of town.

The house, built around 1890, needed a lot of repairs.
Its plaster walls were cracked, its floors warped. The
kitchen and bathroom fixtures were stained and old-
fashioned. But it boasted a huge lot and a garage. Inside,
the house was spacious with room for expansion on the
unfinished second floor and basement.

Best of all, we bought the new house for several thousand dollars less than the price for which we sold our old
house. We were "getting ahead!"

I was eager to begin remodeling this larger house. It
would be so much better for our family. And, if I could
get it finished the way I saw it in my mind, I would be
even prouder of this home than I had been of our first
one.

John had a lot of room in the back yard and in the big
old garage to tinker with machines. I hoped it would be
good therapy for him. John's stress headaches were beginning to worry me. He really disliked the supervisory
position to which he had been elevated and the frustration involved in working in a bureaucracy. I knew he
had been praying and asking the same of others in our
prayer group: If only he could find a job in which he
could be happy.

I sympathized with John. And worried about him. I
encouraged him to look at the bright side of his work.
What more could I do? I was busy with keeping our
family happy and healthy. I expected John to adjust to
bank work eventually just as I had adjusted to mother-

hood after teaching. I had found good things in what had seemed frustrating at first—coming to cherish the freedom being home-employed gave me.

Our second son, Joey, was born in 1975. I was busy with the children and preoccupied, too, with my women's Bible study and the many new friends I was making in our prayer group.

The years slipped by, like sand through my fingers. Occasionally, predictably, John would chafe under the yoke of his bank work.

"Those four walls drive me crazy," he would complain. "I even dread getting out of bed in the morning! If only I could get out of this eight-to-five grind . . . to be my own boss . . . work outside like I always did with Dad on the ranch."

Did his restlessness have anything to do with his age? He was nearly thirty and the thought of facing another ten, twenty, thirty years behind a desk seemed a life too terrible to bear. He agonized for months over whether or not resigning would be irresponsible. To ranchers and farmers like our parents, the insurance and retirement benefits of his bank job were unheard of, easy-money opportunities. Did he dare leave those securities behind? On the other hand, he rationalized, Jesus wouldn't want him tied, like a prisoner, to those securities. At last he took another leap of faith; in the spring of 1978 he resigned.

I wanted John to be happy. A husband's happiness is a wife's happiness. Yet deep down I wasn't sure that John or God knew what they were doing. I was frightened at the thought of leaving all our security behind. How could we know, when we stepped out into a strange, uncertain new world, that Jesus would come with us? How did we know we would be able to walk on water? Or even that Jesus had called us out of the boat? It might not work for us the way it had for Peter. Still, we would never know if it worked until we put our toes in the water.

We were both elated when John was hired as a cement truck driver. Even though the job was far from John's dream of becoming his own boss, it provided the freedom of an outdoor occupation. In the joy of seeing one of John's cherished dreams coming true at last, I momentarily swallowed my fears.

Chapter 4

I'd Rather Be Rich

I drummed my fingers on my taut belly. When I realized what I was doing, I jerked my hands down to my lap. I glanced up to see if anyone had noticed.

No one in the busy restaurant was looking my way. Only my own reflection stared guiltily back at me from the mirror on the opposite wall. I gazed unhappily at my plain face and short brown hair. John always said I was pretty, but I wondered what he would think this morning when he saw my puffy face. The ninth month of my third pregnancy had left its mark, and now I was four long days over my due date. If only I were home where I could stretch my aching legs!

I turned away from the mirror. I looked as if I were sitting in a barrel, peering over the top of my pregnant stomach.

Was Lucille already getting me down? Lucille was an old college friend. Or rather, her husband had been a friend of John's. She was passing through Helena and had asked us to join her at a restaurant for breakfast.

"Oh, Peggy!" Lucille burst through the restaurant

door.

I boosted my swollen body off the plush red leather lounge to greet her.

Lucille bounced across the foyer, looking the part of a bubbling Paris fashion model. Her shining hair swirled bouffantly as she turned her head, then it settled perfectly back into place. Behind her a somber, dark-haired boy followed uncertainly. He clutched a tweed hat in his slim, five-year-old fists.

Lucille's fingers, when she took my hands, were cool and flawlessly manicured.

"Oh, how are you?" Lucille squealed in delight. "You sweet little mother." Her eyes patted my stomach admiringly.

I murmured some appropriate response as Lucille put an arm under my elbow to tow me across the restaurant toward a large corner table.

I tried to sit down gracefully, but scraped my stomach on the table edge, making the water glasses totter. I planted my hands in my lap again. The hastily applied polish on my chipped nails embarrassed me.

"Phillip, you haven't said a word to your Aunt Peggy," Lucille chided, patting the leather seat, asking Phillip to slide closer to her. Hearing Phillip call me "aunt" seemed to please Lucille.

"He's been so eager to see your boys, Peggy. Honestly, the trip out on the plane was ghastly," Lucille rolled her lovely eyes and fluttered her hands as she chatted. "But," she turned to Phillip and her voice took on a brisker cheerfulness, "he's eager to explore Montana and find out how little boys out west behave."

I tried to shove my self-pity aside as I smiled at the

sober, small, Phillip who was unfolding his linen napkin and smoothing it across his knees.

"My boys have been eager to meet you, too. They should be here any moment," I went on, glancing toward the door. I kept my voice deliberately soft, hoping I could hide my crossness under a gentle, quiet mask.

I knew it wasn't fair to dislike Lucille because she was wealthy. It was my own detestable jealousy that was making me uncomfortable, not she.

Jealousy. And yet a lower sin: being suddenly ashamed of John's and my comparative poverty. My pregnancy embarrassed me, too. An obvious sign, I thought, of my lack of control over circumstances. Lucille, however, seemed to flaunt her easy dominance over life.

She had married her husband, Dan, just out of college. He was the son of a Texas cattle rancher, turned oil company executive. Lucille was the only person I knew who had a maid; Phillip, the only child who had a governess. Dan and Lucille made their home in New York, where Dan did something with the stock market.

"Didn't I tell you you'd love Peggy?" Lucille was bubbling to Phillip, more like a sister than a mother, I thought. "Oh, Peggy, if only I were as calm and patient as you!"

Suddenly the restaurant door exploded open and John and our two boys erupted through it.

"Hi, Mom! Hi, Mom!" five-year-old Justin and three-year-old Joey whooped as they gamboled like puppy dogs across the rich pile carpet to me.

John ambled behind them, grinning sheepishly, an apology in his robin's-egg-blue eyes. He was late.

"Oh, they look just like you, John!" Lucille was exclaiming, clasping her hands together in delight and reaching out to hug John's hard, lean body.

John stepped back a bit, his face coloring under his unruly blond hair, his grin deepening. "Good seein' you, Lucille ... Phil," he added, nodding at the little boy.

John bounced down on the seat next to me and slipped an apologetic arm around my swelling waist. He knew how self-conscious I was around Lucille.

I swooped a hand out to catch Joey's chair before it toppled backwards.

Phillip was staring, wide-eyed, at Justin and Joe. I realized at last what gave Phillip such a serious look: his dark brown hair was perfectly in place. My boys' blond fluff bristled in swirls like the down on a duck just out of the water. Phillip's tailored blazer and gabardine slacks contrasted sharply to Justin and Joey's knit striped shirts and denim jeans.

Phillip's polite "How do you do?" stopped the boys' jostling for a moment as they stared curiously at him.

"Say hello to Lucille and Phillip," I urged, a mad desire for these blond miniatures of John to appear well-bred surging in the undercurrent of my voice.

"H'llo." "Hi," they whispered, glancing at me and squirming flat against the backs of their chairs. They hadn't missed my unspoken warning.

"It's nice to meet you, boys," Lucille purred. But I watched her eyes travel from the boys' grimy knuckles and fingernails to their careless, leg-swinging postures. Soap and water had only a short-term effect on my boys.

"Oh!" Lucille gave a little flounce in her chair as the waitress arrived. "Yes, let's order," she commanded us all. "What do the boys like, Peggy? Just order anything.

Of course this breakfast is on me."

I flushed. Don't be so proud, I remonstrated myself. But already I could feel my forced smile retreating again. I answered John's suggestions from the menu in terse monosyllables. What did Lucille know of carefully budgeted meals? I wondered.

"Now, come on, John," Lucille urged cheerfully as the waitress collected our menus and I retreated into my silence across the table. "What's behind all these rumors I've been hearing about you leaving your profession to drive trucks or something?"

John beamed mischievously. "Oh, I just finally took the bull by the horns and did something I should have done years ago," he drawled.

The waitress brought coffee.

Lucille leaned forward, her hazel eyes pleading. "Come on, John," she prodded, "I don't have much time before I have to start the long drive to Dad's ranch. I want to get there before nightfall. Dan and I are both curious about what you're doing. Level with me." Her lips pouted slightly.

John cleared his throat and I knew he was trying to forge his way through natural modesty to express his true feelings. Truck driving was a dream-come-true for John; a manly occupation he had always wanted to call his own. But there was no logic to it financially. It offered none of the insurance or retirement programs he had enjoyed as an accountant. None of the job security either. In Montana driving cement trucks was seasonal work.

John's fingers played with his coffee cup. "Well, you know I was getting a lot of headaches. I don't know—

the office pressures—the hassle—I wanted to be my own boss, independent, working outside where I could breathe a little fresh air. Aw, this cement truck job is only the first step." He patted my knee under the table. I pressed his hand to reassure him.

"Logging is what I really want to get into," he finished, shrugging as if he were describing only a passing fancy he was toying with.

"Logging? You're going into logging?" Lucille spurred him on as the waitress brought steaming platters of hot cakes, sausage, and hashed browns.

"Oh, it's just something I've been looking into." John ducked his head to butter his hot cakes. "Takes a lot of capital to do it right."

"Well, I wish you'd keep Dan and me informed," Lucille told him, "You never know. If it turns out to have some future in it, we might be interested in investing some cash in this logging operation."

My ears burned red. Might be interested in investing some cash, indeed! Joey tucked his napkin under his chin and I snatched it away. Lucille glanced sharply at me.

I sank more deeply into my silence. John reached out to pat my knee again.

He began talking quietly to Lucille, about the economy and Wall Street and whatever other safe topic came to mind.

I choked down my hotcakes, furious that the conversation had ruined my enjoyment of the luxury of breakfast out. Why was I so unreasonably angry?

Lucille's show of wealth and sophistication didn't bother John. He honestly wanted nothing to do with such frivol. Physical labor ("honest hard work", he'd call it) and the out-of-doors gave him as much pleasure as dining out or dreaming of some day owning a new house gave me. I loved him and wanted to allow him the freedom he needed to follow his own dreams. And until now I had been able to squelch my fears about the uncertainty of the path he had chosen for us.

Joey pushed back his half-finished plate and kicked his brother under the table.

I reached for my coat. It was a worn green corduroy car coat I'd had since high school—the only coat in our closet I could button across my bulging middle.

Chapter 5

A Gift for the Journey

A week later our third baby woke me with unmistakable warnings—he was about to join our world.

The hospital was only five miles away from our house. But it was 8:00 a.m. Even in Helena that meant slow rush-hour traffic.

"There's another one!" I muttered through clenched teeth.

John glanced at his watch and gunned the motor. He roared through a yellow light and let out a war cry.

"Ya hoo! Two minutes apart and counting!" he yelled, punching the ceiling of the car with his fist. He grimaced and cradled his wounded knuckles.

The self-pity I had felt in Lucille's company had dissolved in the excitement of the baby arriving at last! My wait was over.

I loved the luxury of having my husband to myself—with no children to interrupt us—even if it was in a speeding car with labor in progress. For that matter, I loved the luxury of a hospital. Soon I would be nestled contentedly in a bed that had buttons to make the head and feet of the bed go up and down. Nurses would pamper me with meals in bed, while I would be responsible for nothing but cuddling my tiny new baby and napping.

John braked the car at the hospital entrance and we proceeded at a fast waddle, to the door.

As patiently as possible, I endured the hospital check-in procedures. At last a smiling blond nurse led me into a labor room where I undressed and slipped into a hospital gown. She examined me quickly.

"You are dilated to three centimeters," she announced cheerfully.

"Thank heaven," I thought. "What a let-down if I had to trudge back home and wait some more!"

The nurse left John and me alone for a minute. John reached for my hand.

"I hope you aren't worrying about how the kids will get along," he implored. "I want you to just relax and think of this as a well-deserved vacation. You know how you're always telling me about the great hospital life . . . breakfast in bed . . . hours of soaking in a hot tub . . . "

I pressed his hand to reassure him. But at John's words a shadow passed over my bright anticipation.

John knew how disappointed I was when the baby hadn't arrived on the due date. My mother had planned to come to take care of the boys while I was hospitalized. But the eighth of May had come and gone with no sign of my delivery. Now, eight days later, when the baby finally was ready, Mom felt she had to stay in North Dakota for my youngest brother's high school graduation. If she had come, I figured the boys would have hardly missed me. But without Mom, they would be shifted around to different girl friends' homes.

"It will work out," John reassured me tenderly, as if he could read my thoughts.

"I know. I'll just have to take it easy when I get home," I replied with fake cheerfulness. The thought of returning to face the work involved with a new baby was enough to make me cry. After three short days in the hospital I would be caught in the busy routine of caring for three children. I dreaded the aftermath more than I dreaded the pain of birth. I wished I could have been babied by my mother until I felt strong again!

At nine o'clock I was jolted out of my martyrdom. The doctor arrived. He checked me and then punctured the membranes of the baby's water sac.

"Might as well wheel her into the delivery room," he told the nurses.

I knew it wouldn't be long. Both Justin and Joey had been born ten minutes after my water had been broken.

Three or four nurses buzzed around me, covering me with sterile cloths and setting out sterile instruments. John was whisked away and draped with a sterile gown.

There it was. The first bearing-down pain seized me and I felt the little head, as hard as a fist-sized rock, slip into the birth canal. I pushed as hard as I could, almost welcoming the pain. The baby is coming! Only a few minutes more!

The first hard contraction passed and I lay back, breathing deeply and trying to rest for the next agonizing push. The doctor seemed to be overly attentive. He kept reaching into the birth canal. Feeling for the baby's head, I supposed.

Again and again the contractions came. I pushed with all my strength until I was sobbing in exhaustion. But still nothing happened.

What's wrong? I wanted to scream at the crowd of blue-gowned nurses and the doctor milling around my feet.

By now the doctor was reaching in, trying to grab the baby's head with each contraction.

He must know I just can't do it, I thought desperately, wetting my dry lips with my tongue and crying out as I tried to push once more.

"What's the matter?" I gasped at last. "Is the baby too big?" I was so exhausted I couldn't open my eyes. I was drenched with sweat. Even my eyelids were wet.

"No, no, she's coming," the doctor soothed me. "We're in no hurry. It's just that it's a girl this time and she's stubborn."

A girl! I tried to comprehend such a thing.

Then the next contraction gripped me and I rallied my weary muscles to push.

"Jesus, Jesus," I heard John whispering at his station near my head. It was so good to have him with me. "What happens if I just can't push her out?" I panicked when the pain loosened its grip. The baby still was not born. But I did find strength from somewhere outside myself to keep trying.

Finally at ten-thirty my squalling eight-pound boy arrived. His battered little head was pointed at the top from the pressures of the birth canal, but, nevertheless, he looked healthy and beautiful.

"It wasn't a stubborn girl," I panted. "It was a stubborn boy."

"He was born posterior, face up instead of face down," the doctor told me. "I kept trying to turn him but he just wouldn't go."

"Oh," was all I felt strong enough to say. I wished he had told me sooner.

The baby yelled lustily as the nurses checked him. The sound filled my ears like music.

Two nurses changed my gown and wheeled me back to my room. I just lay still and let them do all the work. I felt as if I had been steamrolled.

It was over. Back in my room, I lay on my back, propped up by pillows. John tiptoed in, looking intimidated by this white, brisk world. I smiled weakly.

"Well, it's over, Sweetheart," he reassured me, bending down close to my face. "He's beautiful. Do you still want to call him Sam?"

"Uh-huh," I breathed.

"Peggy, are you okay?" John asked, taking my hand and studying me keenly. "Aren't you even going to call your mother?"

"In a little while," I demurred. "Why don't we call the boys?"

"Okay. You tell them," John said, dialing the number of Mary, the neighbor who was watching them.

"Do you think Justin will be disappointed?" I asked softly. "He wanted a baby sister."

"Naw," John shook his head. He handed me the receiver while Mary went to find Justin.

"Hi, Mom," he sounded so young and far away.

"Hi, Honey," I replied, imitating his offhand style. I mustered strength into my voice. "You have a new baby brother."

"Oh," he remarked indifferently. "Well, I guess I have several brothers now."

Such a philosopher, I thought.

Justin was eager to get back to his toys and Joey wasn't interested in the phone. We quickly said good-bye.

"I'll go and let you get some sleep," John whispered, kissing me. "You were great in there."

His encouragement always thrilled me. "Thanks, Darling," I whispered back. "Don't forget to ask when you can come and hold the baby."

"Okay." He winked and left.

"It's so nice to be married to an incurable romantic," I thought, as I lay back on the soft pillow.

A blue gown flew through the air and smacked me in the face. John poked his head in the door.

"Guess what! All I have to do is put that thing over my clothes and I can come in and see little Sam whenever you feed him!"

"Hooray!" I waved sleepily, and he was gone.

After John left I slept gratefully, not waking again until the nurse brought Baby Sam in to be nursed at two o'clock in the afternoon. He was yelling and waving his tiny fists. His little toothless mouth was wide open. Like a bird waiting for the worm, I thought.

The nurse lowered him gently into my arms and he turned his head and began to nurse as soon as I touched his cheek with the nipple. Joy surged through me. Such a healthy baby! Such an eager eater!

How I loved his fat pink skin that fitted his body so loosely. Such strong little legs and pink feet! He had been jostling around inside me for so long I felt we were old friends. I couldn't kiss him enough to satisfy my love.

Little Sam had worn himself out sucking so industriously. He was slumbering deeply in the crook of my arm when John came in, his blue eyes shining. He snatched the blue gown the nurse had given him earlier and slipped his arms into the sleeves. He tied the narrow ribbons impatiently with his broad fingers.

I snickered. "John, you've got the gown on backwards."

He stared at me, then down at the gown hanging open from the satin bow at his Adam's apple to his knees. In a second he waved my foolishness away. "Baloney!" he sniffed good-naturedly.

He scooped up Sammy. Seating himself cross-legged at the foot of my bed, he cooed and clucked at our newest son.

I contentedly watched the two of them. Meticulously John unwrapped the baby to examine every feature, talking softly all the while. Now and then Sam opened one sleepy eye, but he obviously wasn't as thrilled about this first meeting as his father.

"Think he looks like Jussy and Joe?" John asked me. "Was their hair this dark at first?"

I wrinkled my nose in thought and nodded.

Outside a spring shower was pelting the street and soaking the grass and flowers. I knew the cement company boss where John worked had been happy to give him the day off. There weren't many cement jobs in this rainy weather.

Already, a month and a half into the cement truck job, we were learning that, as the newest driver, John was the first to be sent home early when it rained. The future promised nothing better. The cement business would grind to a halt in the fierce Montana winter.

Where would this frightening new road lead us? The additional expense of the baby wouldn't make the journey easier. But something in me insisted that a baby could only be a gift, not a burden.

"Please, Lord," I implored as I watched the raindrops pelt my window, "I have to believe You are with us or I'll die of panic. Let it all really be a part of Your plan for us. And this innocent baby ... in a way he's like Your gift for the journey. Let him be the beacon that helps us find the way."

John's eyes followed mine to the window. "Let it rain." He grinned his familiar boyish grin. "I didn't want to work today anyway."

I smiled. "You are right where you belong today," I assured him, forcing away my fears for what seemed like the millionth time.

Sam gurgled in agreement.

Chapter 6

Freedom Knows No Bounds

I glanced up from the diapers I was folding on the top step of the front porch and applauded Justin—riding his bicycle without training wheels.

"Look, Mom," he called, wobbling down the sidewalk. Justin braked to a shrieking stop at the bottom of the porch steps. He nearly plummeted over the handle bars into my lap.

An indignant Joey followed Justin around the curve in the sidewalk. His square little knees flew up and down as he pedaled his tricycle in fury.

"I could go as fast as Jus if you'd take my training wheels off, too!" he announced hotly, ramming the cement porch step with his front tricycle tire.

I stifled a smile and swept the diapers off my lap to make room for Joey. How would I explain that the two rear wheels on a tricycle are not as disposable as bicycle training wheels?

"Beep-beep!" John drove up in our Subaru station

wagon and parked at the curb.

"Daddy's here! Daddy's here!" Justin and Joey chanted. They dismounted their cycles and scrambled to the gate. I sighed and ambled after the boys. It was only two o'clock in the afternoon. Even though there was no rain today the company must have run out of cement orders and sent John home.

I watched as John whirled each of the boys around and tossed them, shrieking, into the air. He was such a good father. And all my fears about having no one to help me with the baby had proven unfounded. Because of the rain John hadn't had to work while I was in the hospital. He'd been home every day with the boys. Justin and Joey hadn't appeared to miss me at all; they were elated with Daddy's undivided attention for three days. Then, when I'd come home and the weather had cleared, a different girl friend called every morning, offering to come and get Justin and Joe and watch them for the day. It was as if some Master Planner had scheduled all my babysitting.

Sam was two weeks old. My old energies were swarming back, but so were my old worries. I fretted about making our money stretch if the cement company didn't give John more hours.

John cinched an arm around my waist and we strolled back to the porch steps. The boys raced away, around the house.

"Well," he sighed with a wry smile, "looks like we'd better start looking into that firewood sale in earnest."

A hard knot twisted in the pit of my stomach as I picked up my stack of diapers from the top porch step. It had been frightening enough to leave the security of the bank to go to a job whose pay depended on how favorable the weather was. But our next alternative was downright terrifying! It would mean cutting firewood from a timber sale the U. S. Forest Service had put up for bid. Logging the wood and selling it would be more than a full-time job for John. But I had qualms about how realistic we were being in gambling with such an unknown occupation. Nearly everyone I knew trekked to the woods for their own firewood; no one bought it from a vendor. After John had gathered firewood for the entire summer, we wouldn't know if we could sell enough even to buy staples like peanut butter and jelly. What if we lost all our savings? Could I bite my tongue and go on acting brave if we started dipping into that?

"Knock! Knock!" Justin singsonged to his dad, dropping beside him on the bottom porch step. I swallowed hard and gathered my diapers again.

"Who's there?" John singsonged back to Justin.

"Lettuce."

"Lettuce who?" John asked in mock anticipation.

"Lettuce be friends!" Justin shouted, triumphantly. He and Joey giggled, wrinkling their freckled noses and showing their even white baby teeth, as John fell off the step backwards in surprise. The boys bounded around the corner of the house again, jostling and shouting.

"It's just not working," John muttered softly, growing serious once more as he dropped down on the bottom porch step. "We can't live on nothing. There just aren't enough cement jobs with all this rain."

I reached down to pat John's sun-bleached hair, warm from the heat of the sun.

"Guess I'll go talk to the Forest Service boys," John

continued, brightening slightly. "Maybe we've just got to bite the bullet and really strike out on our own. . . . Hey, I heard about a guy with a workhorse for sale up in Wolf Creek."

"Oh, really?" I asked, a flicker of hope warming me on the inside. John's optimism was catching. Wolf Creek was only thirty miles away. John had talked of logging with a workhorse because it was so much cheaper than buying a caterpillar and other modern logging equipment. However, using workhorses, like vending firewood, was not commonly done any more. Although John had been keeping his ear to the ground, we hadn't heard of a single workhorse for sale in the area.

Joey came scurrying back across the yard. He made me think of an awkward, rolypoly puppy dog when he ran. If only spring days could last forever. I loved the smell of damp earth and new grass; the sight of my son running over the grass to me, a chubby package of love and innocence, his blue eyes shining with mischief.

"Knock knock," he tittered, landing in a heap in John's lap.

John rolled his eyes in fun. Joey was doing a three-year-old's imitation of his big brother's hilarious joke.

"Who's there?" John chimed.

Joey paused to think, chewing his lower lip.

Then he clapped his hands, remembering.

"Salad," he shouted.

We all whooped and laughed in surprise. Joey, pleased with his successful joke, ran off to find Justin.

I was determined not to tell John of my fears in the weeks that followed. He was busy talking to Forest Service people and others in an attempt to get a firewood business going. I wanted to be a supportive wife and I knew my doubts would only cast a dampening shadow on his hopes. John was a hard worker and did anything he set his mind to well. Furthermore, I had confidence in his good judgment. I forced my nagging fears into the back of my mind and concentrated on my faith in John.

In a way, I didn't have much choice but to encourage him in his search for an alternative job. We simply couldn't live on the pay he received from the few hours' work at the cement company; we might as well try something else. Besides, I assured myself, if things didn't get better John could find another accounting job. On the surface, I believed he'd be willing to return to the office.

John talked to some realtors and put an ad in the paper to try to find land to lease for our firewood business. We planned to call it The Woodyard. But none of the property we looked at suited our purposes. Most of the small plots of land were covenanted against commercial enterprises. Others were much too expensive.

After about three weeks we found a three-bedroom home on two acres of ground. It was zoned for commercial use. It cost only ten thousand dollars more than we could ask for our home in Helena. The house delighted me. Being only a year old, everything in it shined clean and new. Best of all, there was an extra bathroom, something I regarded as the height of luxury for our growing family.

The larger payments were a concern, of course. But somehow John and I hoped to swing them. We signed a buy-sell on the house—the seller would hold the house for thirty days, giving us time to find a buyer for our own home.

I prayed it wouldn't take long for us to sell. "I'll go crazy if I have to keep this house immaculate for prospective customers for a whole month," I thought, surveying the freshly vacuumed living and dining rooms. Joey had toddled behind the vacuum, leaving such a trail of Cheerios that it looked as if the "Cheerios Kid" had rip-snorted through.

Meanwhile, John signed a lease with the Forest Service for some timber land about twenty-five miles from Helena. At last, we had the firewood; everything was falling into place. We even found a buyer for our silver bullion, supplying us with badly needed cash.

On June 15th John quit driving cement trucks. He spent his work days buying logging equipment and getting it ready to bring in the wood.

John spotted a newspaper ad for an old logging trailer that could be pulled with a pickup. I invited myself and the boys along on the seventy-mile drive over to pick up the trailer.

A golden collie roused himself from his bed on the front porch as we pulled up to the ranch house. He thumped his tail twice as John stepped over him to knock on the screen door. Flies droned lazily in the shade of the golden willow tree where John had parked our truck.

Several minutes passed before a lean, bent rancher came to the door and spoke to John. He gestured off toward the parched pasture and then retreated back into the house.

"He isn't coming with us?" I prodded, as John steered the truck through a pole gate out toward the pasture where the trailer sweltered in the sun.

"He says he has emphysema," John replied quietly. "He can't be away from his oxygen tank for more than a few minutes an hour."

We found the trailer. John seemed pleased with it. The heavy iron frame had not been hurt by the years it had stood there unprotected in the grass. The tires had weather-checked; web-shaped cracks were etched into their sidewalls. But John said they had good tread.

The blistering heat was beginning to make me dizzy. The boys, who had whooped in triumph when John allowed them to ride the short distance from the ranch house on the back of the truck, were complaining now of thirst and mosquito bites.

John hooked the trailer to the truck and hauled it out of its bed in the pasture to the ranch house yard.

"The rancher has a wife," John told me, once more parking the truck in the shade by the ranch house. "You might want to go in and visit with her." I shot him a withering glance. Meeting strangers was much more painful to me than to him.

"Well, it's going to take a while to get these lights and brakes wired," he warned. I didn't dream he meant four hours.

I gathered up Baby and spread a blanket for him in the grass under the golden willow. I sat down in the shade to watch the boys playing with the collie.

Soon the rancher's wife came out and offered us cool drinks inside. The boys didn't wait for a second invitation. I followed more slowly, cradling Sam's hot little body against my own.

Her name was Alice, she said. Her hair was graying, curled neatly in short ringlets. Her slim body was hard and strong in a white overblouse and blue jeans.

The inside of her house repelled me. Dust coated the wooden tables and outlined paths of footprints on the unpainted floors.

Alice seated us in her living room. I laid a blanket between Baby Sam and the threadbare upholstered couch.

The boys sipped the cold lemonade and whirled one another around in the swivel armchair by the grimy roll-top desk.

"It's a bit dusty in here," Alice apologized as if reading my thoughts. "It's him," she jerked her head toward the kitchen where the wheeze of an oxygen machine pulsed monotonously. "He won't let me dust. Says it just sends all the particles into the air and chokes him." She shrugged. But her eyes had turned hard with suppressed rage. I didn't blame her. How could she endure living in such a mess? Surely the two of them could have worked out a compromise—something to stem the bitterness pounding inside her.

"Hey!" the man yelled from the kitchen, "I'm waitin' on my lunch!" I never heard him address her with any name but "Hey."

Alice pressed her colorless lips together tightly, but she did not retort.

"Come on out to the kitchen," she urged me. "I have his lunch all ready."

To my surprise the crotchety fellow held out his hand to shake mine and nodded for me to sit down in a straight-backed wooden kitchen chair across the table from him.

"See this here machine?" he demanded. He gestured

disparagingly toward the gasping oxygen machine. "It's owned me for seventeen years."

I did feel sorry for him. No wonder the old man was cranky—how frustrating to be a captive of a wheezing machine. His voice droned on through the afternoon heat, listing his slate of grievances against the world. Alice was silent. I sensed hatred pulsating between them: something big and awful—too awful for them to let out, but eating their insides while they held it in. When had their frustration turned on each other? Had they seen it start to happen and not been able to stop it?

The sun still sweltered when John finished his work on the trailer and we climbed back into the truck. Fear sweltered in me, too. Fear for what John and I could become. I was scared of the little flickers of resentment at John that I felt on days like today when his need for a logging trailer had landed the kids and me in this hot, dusty war zone for four long hours. How long till his dreams and my fears made a war between us—me scared and resenting his brave forward strides—he dauntless and fighting my holding him back. Oh, I could never bear to lose John that way! I must believe in him and support his endeavors. But what would I do if I felt a wall starting to form, hard and angry inside me? Could I fight that? I didn't know.

Chapter 7

A Horse on the Roof

A few days later, on a cool summer morning, we drove our three-quarter-ton pickup truck to Wolf Creek to get the workhorse.

"There he is," Justin breathed in awe as we lurched up to the corrals by the barn.

There stood the biggest horse I had ever seen. I was alarmed. Those gigantic hooves could effortlessly trample one of my little boys to death! To me, the enormous beast was raw, uncontrolled power personified. How could we entrust our livelihood, our very lives, to his untamed strength?

John got out. He and McFarland, the owner, inspected the horse, running their hands over his huge hindquarters and leg muscles; then threw a harness on him and John drove him around the corral. Justin watched in open admiration from the corral fence. I leaned on the rail, praying for wisdom for John. Try as he might, he had never turned me into a cowgirl. This horse-logging business would rely entirely on John's skills. Joey wriggled in between me and the rail, pushing my knees away from the fence and hollering to be hoisted up beside Justin.

"Can we see him pull?" I heard John ask.

"Ah, sure. Let's see if there is a singletree in the barn there," McFarland suggested. A singletree, or a doubletree with a team of horses, is a metal bar to which the tug-lines of the harness are fastened. Chains are run from the singletree and hooked onto the load the horse is to pull.

They disappeared into the barn but returned in a few moments empty-handed. McFarland and John hunted around the barnyard for another half hour or so.

"Should have something somewhere here to hitch 'im up," the bowlegged rancher kept muttering.

"Well, that's okay." John finally gave up.

McFarland straightened his lean shoulders. "Well, I'd 'a liked you to seen him pull," he attested cheerfully. "But I can assure you you'll be pleased with 'im. Good horse. Yep, a good worker."

John raised his eyebrows at me but said nothing, as he trotted by to jump in the truck. He backed it around to the loading ramp.

My misgivings only increased as John tried to lead the horse into the truck. The balky beast refused to step on the ramp. Eventually McFarland strolled down the lane to a small bunkhouse and ambled back with two lanky ranchhands. All four men bent down to push against the horse's hindquarters. Grunting and heaving, they were able to throw him off balance enough so that he would take a step forward. Inch by inch they forced him up the ramp and into the truck.

The top of the horse's back stood at least a foot higher

than the top of the stockrack on our truck. I caught my breath when I saw his powerful head looming over the top of our truck cab. He shuffled nervously from one foot to the other while the little truck rocked under his weight.

"Surely riding in the truck with that animal right over us isn't as dangerous as it looks," I told myself.

The men all ambled back to the corral. They each hooked a boot heel over the lower rail, their elbows over the top one, and leaned back to gaze with satisfied airs at the horse.

"Yep, he'll do you fine," McFarland proclaimed, punctuating with a spit of snoose that splattered with precision on the hub of our left rear tire.

John signed the check for $950 and handed it to McFarland. They shook hands and we all piled into the truck.

The boys clambered to poke their heads out the window to see the horse. John grabbed them and stuffed them back into the cab.

I kept eyeing John, silently pleading for a sign indicating that he had come to his senses—hoping he would order us all back out of the truck. But he seemed confident, even excited about his new purchase. The boys chatted eagerly about the horse and how they were going to be cowboys as we eased to a start.

"Don't worry, Dad," Justin reassured his father, "if you ever get hit by a tree, I'll jump on this horse and ride to town faster than any truck and get help."

"I don't know, Jus," Joey countered, wrinkling his sunburned nose in concentration. "That's an awful big horse to get on all by yourself."

"Aw, I could do it," Justin replied, placing his hands on his hips indignantly. "I'd just climb up on the truck and jump down on the horse's back when he ran by."

I glanced nervously at John. We had turned in a wide circle, then driven slowly down the long driveway to the highway. John glanced into the rearview mirror as the truck jolted slightly. The horse seemed to be throwing his weight from side to side.

John caught my eye and winked. "It'll be okay. He's tied in so he can't go anywhere. Horses are just like people. They don't like to move." John went on, warming to the subject as the boys stopped their chatter to listen to him. "Horses can become very good friends with each other. Now this fellow has lived here for a long time and knows these other horses really well. He's maybe never been off this ranch before. You can understand why he's nervous about leaving. But he'll soon be over it."

We were on the highway and picking up speed now. We all listened to the heavy thumps of the horse's hooves as he moved about in the truck box. John's grip on the wheel was tight, but nonetheless the little truck veered now and then as the horse shifted his weight.

Just as we turned a corner and the ranch disappeared from sight behind us, there was a wild thumping in the back of the truck. Suddenly the truck lurched to one side. Now the thumping was everywhere, even on the roof.

"My Lord, he's trying to jump." John yelled, fighting with the wheel as the truck careened toward the ditch. He braked hard and the little truck shivered to a stop. John jumped out of the truck as the truck box seemed to explode in a torrent of violent kicks.

The boys stared at me, their blue eyes wide with fright, but I didn't move.

"Daddy will have everything under control in a minute," I assured them calmly. And, strangely enough, with John spurred into action, I believed we were out of danger. What worried me was the possibility that $950 of our precious savings had just strangled itself.

"Get the kids and get out of the truck!" John thundered at me as he started cautiously up the stockracks.

Justin sprang out his dad's door. I clambered out the other door, cradling the baby under one arm and dragging Joe behind me with the other. We ran down the road for nearly fifty yards before I dared stop. The three boys were howling.

I looked back. The horse had reared up, throwing his front legs over the top of the stockrack and onto the top of the cab. He would have jumped over the top if his head hadn't been tied down by John's halter rope. Somehow he had wedged his right front hoof back between the two top rails of the stockrack. The horse thrashed wildly, panic-stricken, as his hoof remained securely trapped.

I could hear John's voice, soothing the sweating, wild-eyed giant. I squeezed my eyes shut as John cautiously reached over to free the trapped hoof. I could feel hot tears against my eyelids.

Impatient with my tears, I rubbed my eyes and peered at John.

John tugged and tugged again, but the huge hoof was too large to slip through the rails. How long before the horse started bolting and kicking again?

Joey's hand on my shoulder was shaking and I hugged him tighter against me. Baby Sammy let out a piercing wail. I realized my own hands were trembling as I tried to comfort my babies.

"It's all right. Everything's okay now," I heard myself murmuring over and over as I reached out to hug Justin, too, into the circle of my arm. My voice quavered.

"I'm going to have to cut a chunk out of the rail," John called over his shoulder. "Stay where you are in case he starts acting up again!"

I felt Justin stiffen against my arm. John slowly climbed down the rack.

I could hear him talking softly to the horse as he rummaged through the tools and ropes and other paraphernalia on the floor of the truck cab. In a moment he tipped the truck seat forward and dug in the space behind the seat.

At last, with a grunt, he produced an old, bent hacksaw blade. He cautiously mounted the racks again.

"Jesus take care of him," I pleaded inwardly. I bit my lip.

John was still quietly talking to the horse. He eased the saw blade carefully to the rack near the trapped hoof and painstakingly cut a six-inch section out of the top rack.

I could see him stretch down to loosen the halter rope, at the same time lifting the trapped hoof through the cut rack and onto the top of the cab.

Sensing his freedom, the horse reared back, lifting both front legs up and over the rack and back down onto the truck bed. He stood quietly now, a shudder of pure exhaustion rippling through his wet muscles.

"Dad's got him happy again," Joey whispered.

A sigh quivered involuntarily out of my throat. I hadn't realized I had been holding my breath.

The horse had gone berserk. He could have come crashing through the truck cab and killed us all! Our safety, our very lives, had been in jeopardy! I had never felt so utterly helpless.

"Lord," I prayed, "how can I get back in that truck and ride thirty more miles with my babies in danger? Nothing seems safe anymore. How can I go on living day by day with nothing secure to hold onto? We've left a predictable, safe world to make a living with this wild, powerful beast! Where has it led us—to buying a horse that will kill us all? Is that the price we'll have to pay for gambling that a different life will make John happy?"

I didn't expect an answer, but it came. In my mind a thought took shape and overpowered my thoughts. I knew the words came from someone and someplace outside of me:

"You have made a mistake. You have the wrong horse. This is a hard road to follow and you will make more mistakes. But I will be with you to lead you through it all."

John drove the truck slowly toward us. The head of the exhausted horse loomed over the cab.

John pulled to a stop beside us and strode around to where we were huddled beside the road. He opened the passenger door and boosted the boys inside. They chatted excitedly, unafraid, in their father's strong presence.

John turned around and hugged me. "I'm sorry," he said. I let him hold me for a few moments. I didn't know what to say.

"The horse is calmed down now," John said quietly. "I have his head tied down to such a short rope that he can't lunge like that again. We'll take it slow. Are you okay now?"

"No. I'm scared to death!"

John's shoulders sagged.

"Oh, I didn't mean that! I'm all right!" I relented. I pecked him on the neck.

I sensed that he was as frightened as I. I mustn't falter and undermine his show of confidence. Our whole little family was leaning heavily on John's strength.

I set my jaw firmly as I settled back into the seat for the long ride home. I could see there was more to worry about on our strange new journey than money. Like innocents forging a trail up some steep wilderness mountain, we were on a dangerous path. Our very lives could be at stake. I clung to the hope that the powerful "thought" I had sensed on the road was from Jesus.

Chapter 8

Another Horse, Another Chance

The next afternoon, as I swept some wet spaghetti around the kitchen floor, Joey sauntered by. He smelled strongly of the maple syrup that had been stuck in his hair since breakfast. His sticky hands carried a stack of dirty plates from the dishwasher toward the living room. Before I could catch him, the phone rang, and Justin wailed from the bathroom, "Mo-o-o-om! My loose tooth just came out and went down the drain! Mo-o-om! I'm BLEEDING!"

"I have a collect call for anyone from John Brooke," a telephone operator said blandly. "Will you accept the call?"

"Er-r . . . yes, yes," I stammered. My mouth went dry. What had happened now? John must be calling from the little country store in Canyon Creek. It was located just below the firewood sale, about twenty miles away.

"Peggy?"

"John, what's the matter?"

"It's the horse. Call the bank and put a stop-payment on the check."

"What happened? What's the matter?" I demanded. I closed my eyes and thrust a finger in my free ear. Sammy was howling. Justin was tugging at my sleeve, moaning with his hand over his mouth. Joey trudged in from the living room for another load of dirty plates. How could I concentrate?

"Lord," I prayed, "protect us! Protect our $950."

"The horse just won't pull," John said softly on the other end of the line. He sounded as if he could hardly speak the words without crying. "I've been working and working with him, but he won't even try. Call the bank right away and I'll take him back up to Wolf Creek as fast as I can."

"But what if they've already cashed ... " I protested, but the connection went dead.

I hung up the phone and hustled Justin and Joey into their bedroom. I handed each one a toy, planted howling Sammy in his cradle, stuffed Joey's plates under one arm, and scurried back to the kitchen to dial the bank.

A woman answered.

She pleasantly transferred my call to the right department, where the stop-payment was handled effortlessly. I was relieved that no one appeared to suspect me of doing something illegal.

John drove the horse back to Wolf Creek without stopping at home. McFarland was away. John carefully explained the situation to one of the lanky cowboys down at the barn and left the horse in the corral. To our relief, McFarland never tried to cash the check.

John continued to cut down trees at the firewood sale.

Every night he scanned the paper to find another horse. It was almost a week before he heard of a draft-horse show. At this event, draft-horse owners from Montana and other nearby states pitted their horses against one another in pulling contests.

We packed up diapers and children and headed for Hamilton, some 180 miles away. The grandstands were full, the pulling contest in progress, when we arrived.

I had never seen such draft horses! They dwarfed McFarland's horse. They shamed him with their beauty. Huge flaxen-colored Belgian horses strained against their loads. Then came the powerful Clydesdales, sinewy muscles flexing their shining red hindquarters. Silky streams of hair formed the fetlocks that rippled gracefully over their mighty hooves. Last of all were the dappled-gray Percherons. Their broad necks rose from massive, muscular shoulders, giving them an aura of rugged, untamed strength.

The horses pulled in teams of two. Each team pulled an iron sled loaded with hay bales a distance of about twenty feet. Then more bales were added and each team again had a turn to pull the load. Still more bales were tossed on the sled until only the winning team could pull the load the distance of twenty feet without stopping. If a team started, stopped, and started again, they were disqualified.

Not only was I impressed with the power of these massive animals, I was struck by some teams' eagerness to pull. They seemed to sense the excitement of the crowd. Some drivers leaned their whole weight against the drive lines to hold the horses down to a slow trot as they approached the load to which they would be hitched.

"Look, John," I whispered, pointing to a team of Clydesdales that was being backed up to the load. "They're so excited they look like they're stepping on hot coals!" No sooner was a hoof on the ground than it was back in the air. They seemed to be slowly trotting in place.

The doubletree was securely hooked to the load at last and the driver gave his team their head. The horses hit their collars and snapped against the tug-lines, which cracked like a rifle shot under the weight.

"Now this is the team to watch," John told me, pointing to a pair of cream-colored Belgians who were next in line.

"Why them?" I asked, confused. They seemed awfully quiet to me.

"Watch!" John silenced me, peering intently as the Belgians were driven into position. They were so calm there was actually a slack in their drive lines.

Several other men sprang forward to help hold the team as the driver whistled for them to back up to the load. He waved the men away.

"Will you look at that?" John breathed in amazement as the driver dropped the reins and bent over to hook up the load. The horses waited quietly.

Now the driver was ready. He spoke to the team. Shoulder to shoulder, the two horses eased their weight into their collars. There was no snap of the tug-lines, only the creak of leather and a jingle of chains. But the load was moving steadily the twenty-foot distance.

"That's the kind of horse we need," John whispered excitedly. "One that moves slowly into the load instead of lunging and breaking up harness. Start praying that we can find something that works as well as those Belgians."

"Ah," I nodded.

The Belgians John liked so well lost out to another team of Belgians and a team of Clydesdales.

"That's okay," John said, as he lifted Justin and Joey in his arms, "third place is pretty good."

I followed him through the crowd and toward the car. Baby Sam was asleep in my arms.

"I'll be back as soon as I can," John said at the car, and he disappeared into the warm summer night.

"Oh, Jesus," I sighed as Justin and Joe settled down under blankets in the back of our station wagon, "lead him through this crowd to just the right horse." I nursed Baby Sam while the grandstand crowd milled around our car on foot or roared by in a flash of headlights from four-wheel drive vehicles. The horse trailers all seemed to be leaving. Had we come all this way for nothing?

Meanwhile, John had sprinted across the arena where he came upon only one man leading a Clydesdale horse across the dimly lit field. The other horsemen had all disappeared in the darkness.

John introduced himself. "I'm looking for someone with a good, low-keyed workhorse for sale," John told him. I'm starting a firewood business. The sticks are small so I don't need a large horse. In fact, I hear that what a man wants in the woods is a smaller, short-coupled horse who can maneuver well in and out of tight spots."

"Well, I may have just the horse you're looking for," Mr. Odegaard responded amicably. "He's a seven-year-old Clydesdale gelding, short-coupled, and not over-large. In fact, I'd say he weighs right around 1800 pounds. He's not a charger; just a good steady puller."

"How much would you need to have for him?" John asked.

"One thousand dollars," Mr. Odegaard replied. They agreed to meet at the stockyard in Dillon, Montana, the next Sunday morning. Dillon was about two hundred miles southwest of Helena, halfway between Mr. Odegaard's ranch in Idaho Falls and Helena.

When John returned to the car the boys were all asleep. It was eleven o'clock at night. On the way home, John related his story.

"How do we know this horse will be any good?" I demanded.

"Well, we don't," John retorted. "But I figure it's all we can do. I told him I want to see the horse pull before I buy him. I trust the guy," he added quietly.

After the last catastrophe I didn't want to trust any-one, but it seemed I had no choice. We couldn't log with-out a horse.

It was 2:00 a.m. when we tumbled, exhausted, into our bed. "M-m-m," I murmured, cuddling up to John. "Nothing feels as good as our own bed." I wondered if there was any greater luxury anywhere than smooth, clean sheets and a not-too-soft mattress and that drowsy feeling pulling me down—down—down.

"I'm glad I married you," John whispered, turning around to hug me warmly.

"Me, too." It was one of our favorite love-phrases. To

be glad we married said it all. Before we were married, how hard it had been to say good-night and part. As man and wife, this time of day—the warmth and security and being-loved feeling of falling asleep in each others' arms and knowing we could stay—always seemed like frosting on a cake.

Two days later John and Justin left early in the morning for Dillon. John had loaded the stockracks back on the truck. I prayed as I watched them rattle out of the yard.

"Oh, Lord, let this horse ride home quietly." What were the chances that this horse would be a good logger? I tried not to think.

John's truck broke down thirty miles out of Helena. He worked frantically for an hour on the engine, worrying all the while that he would miss Mr. Odegaard. At last John did get the truck repaired and continued on his way.

When John finally reached Dillon, he pulled into the Cenex gas station and asked for directions to the stockyard.

"Which one?" the attendant responded, "There's one in the middle of town and one ten miles out toward Idaho."

Rather than lose precious time looking for the stockyard in town John headed back out to the highway. He would check the out-of-town stockyard first. If Odegaard wasn't there, John could retrace the highway back to town and keep his eyes peeled for a truck with Idaho plates pulling a horse trailer. If only Odegaard hadn't gotten tired of waiting and headed back to Idaho!

John was approaching the ten-mile highway marker,

studying the landscape nearby for a sign of the stock-yards, when a truck pulling a horse trailer on the front-age road caught his eye.

Thinking he should check the truck out, John braked and swung off the highway onto a little approach. He backed his truck around and followed the other truck about half a mile before the driver turned off the road into a stockyard.

It was Mr. Odegaard! He had had a delay and was an hour late, as well.

"From that moment I began praising God that He had everything carefully laid out for us," John told me later.

Odegaard's Clydesdale was smaller than the horses John had seen at the pulling contest.

"I'll show you how he pulls," Mr. Odegaard assured John.

The horse stood quietly while he was harnessed.

"There's a singletree hanging on the far side of the trailer," Odegaard told John as he led the Clydesdale over to the front of our truck.

Justin walked cautiously over to rub the horse's nose. Odegaard took the singletree from John, attached it to the tug-lines and hooked it onto the front bumper of the truck.

"Okay, climb in and put 'er in neutral," Mr. Odegaard ordered John.

"C'mon, Jus," John called as he climbed behind the wheel of the truck. "Let's go for a ride."

John shifted the truck out of gear and watched as the horse easily and quietly pulled the truck forward and stopped at Mr. Odegaard's command.

"Now shift 'er into low," Mr. Odegaard called. John

moved the gearshift into first. Again the horse obediently threw his weight into the collar. To John's surprise and Justin's delight, the truck was moving again.

"Some horse!" John murmured in awe.

"Yeah," Justin breathed, "he's sure strong to move this big truck."

"All right," Odegaard commanded, "leave 'er in gear and set your emergency brake and we'll see how he does."

"Are you sure?" John balked. He didn't want to hurt this valiant little horse.

"Yup!" Odegaard replied.

This time the Clydesdale strained against the load. His hindquarters dropped, the muscles tightened under his glossy red hide. The truck began to move!

"Whoa!" Mr. Odegaard grunted.

John bounded out of the truck. He had grown up with stock horses, but never dreamed that a workhorse could have such strength.

"He's one pullin' horse!" John exulted.

"He's hard-working," Mr. Odegaard allowed. "I'll stand behind him that he'll pull good for you." The deal was closed.

John had built a four-foot long ramp that was hinged to the back of the truck. It doubled as the back gate of the stockrack when it was in the upward position. Now John strode around to the back of the truck to let down the ramp.

"Think he'll go up this ramp okay?" asked John, remembering the trouble he had had loading McFarland's horse.

"Yeah, he should," replied Mr. Odegaard.

John walked halfway up the ramp before turning to take the halter rope from Mr. Odegaard.

"Oh, no," exclaimed Mr. Odegaard, "No need for you to be up there!"

John obediently jumped down from the ramp.

Mr. Odegaard led the Clydesdale to the foot of the ramp. He draped the halter rope over the horse's muscular neck and grunted softly to him.

Our Clydesdale nimbly trotted up the ramp and into the truck. John looked up to see Justin's eyes shining as he gazed from the back window of the cab at his horse. Boy and horse were nose-to-nose through the glass.

We never regretted buying the Clyde. He lived up to everything Mr. Odegaard had promised.

As I thought about each coincidence that had led us to find the Clydesdale, I remembered the "thought" that had come over me beside the road from Wolf Creek: " . . . I will be with you to lead you through it all."

What a comfort to think that trusting God was sufficient, but I wondered: could I do it again when the next obstacle presented itself? Old habits, I knew, were hard to break.

Chapter 9

Team on a Runaway!

By this time we had our house ready for market. We advertised it in the paper and immediately a young couple came to our doorstep. As I led them through the house they didn't ask many questions, and showed only mild interest. I was closing the door of the old log garage when the woman smiled and said, "Well, I guess you've just sold your house."

"You mean you want it?" I asked, amazed.

"It's just what we've been looking for," the husband replied without hesitation.

They gave me $350 earnest money and said they would be in touch after they talked to their banker.

I was stunned by how nicely everything in our lives was now falling into place! Wasn't God good!

As I watched the young couple drive away, the voiceless assurance again came into my mind. "Remember all I have led you safely through that you may keep faith later, when things get rough. I am with you always." This time I knew that God had spoken the words.

"Oh, Lord, thank You!" I prayed, my heart overflow-

ing with gratitude. I turned the burner on under the tea-
kettle and, while I talked to Jesus, brewed myself a relaxing cup of tea.

"We blundered so badly on that first horse, Lord, but
You protected us and our money. Now You've sold our
house in the wink of an eye. You didn't make me waste
any time on the wrong customers. Thank You!"

That evening, when John came in from the woods and
saw the earnest money check, he let out a whoop. "You
mean they just decided they wanted the house right on
the spot?" He asked me over and over for the details.
"They wrote out a check just like that? Didn't even dick-
er on the price?"

"Yes . . . yes . . . no," I laughed.

We were ecstatic! Yet, as I climbed into bed that night,
I felt the joy receding. Now that our house was sold,
buying the new one was nearly a reality. What if we
couldn't handle the larger payments on the new house?
After all, this logging business was untried. It certainly
hadn't produced any income for us yet.

The next two days I agonized. How were we going to
pay for the new house? Our old house payments were
less than one hundred dollars a month. The new payments would be over three hundred dollars. Where
would the extra money come from? What had happened
to my faith—so strong just days before? I didn't know
the answers to any of my questions and neither did John.
Whenever I voiced my concerns to him, he just shrugged
them off.

"We can't have The Woodyard in the middle of
town," he reminded me. "That house and the two acres
was the only property we could find to put a commercial

enterprise on, remember?"

He sighed. "If I have to start looking for a second job, I will. But for now we'll just keep moving ahead."

John was right, of course. Yet I couldn't stop worrying. I tortured myself with visions of our going broke and losing everything.

Early the third morning, someone knocked on the front door. I extracted Joey, who was trying to rescue an ant from the swift fate of my broom, from the dust pile on the kitchen floor, and then answered the door.

"Hi," I said cheerfully to the young man who had just bought our house.

"Hi," he mumbled. "Um . . . I'm really sorry about this. I mean . . . we really like your house . . . but we talked to the bankers and we just can't afford the payments." He cleared his throat, his eyes flicking across my face and then down to the floor. "I mean, we'd really be getting ourselves in too deep."

My heart sank all the way to my shoes. My worry about our increased payments evaporated. Now all I could foresee was the great effort in putting the house back on the market and keeping it spotless for more prospective buyers. "Oh no, Lord, I thought You had handled this so neatly!" I moaned inwardly.

The young man looked as if he wanted to cry in embarrassment.

"Oh, that's okay, no big deal," I heard myself assuring him.

"Do you think there's any chance we might get our earnest money back?" he asked, a glimmer of hope leaping into his eyes.

My heart went out to him. My disappointment wasn't

his fault.

"Of course," I said. I escaped into the bedroom to find my checkbook. But I was fighting tears. I yearned for the days when life had been predictable.

"Why can't anything go easily?" I muttered to myself. "And as for You, God," I sort of whispered in my mind so as not to make Him too mad, "I thought You were going to make everything go right for us!"

"There you are," I murmured graciously. The young man ran down the front steps two at a time. I trudged slowly out to the back yard to tell John and the boys.

They had just returned from the grocery store. The car was jammed to the roof with banana boxes for us to pack in when we moved.

"Look at how many boxes we got stuffed in here!" Justin yelled when he saw me. I watched glumly while the boys and John heaped the boxes into the old coal bin in the basement.

Then, as the boys tore outside to check the car for more boxes, I drew John aside to tell him of our misfortune. We decided not to say anything to the children. After all, as John assured me, someone else would come along soon and buy the house.

About two weeks later the Forest Service manager called John offering a contract on a saw-log sale. There had been a "blow-down"—a violent windstorm twisting through a bunch of trees, knocking seventy-five-foot trees down as if they were matchsticks. The trees were in a small area called the Priest Camp and were surrounded by numerous summer cabins.

The Forest Service particularly wanted John to log the trees—because we had a horse. Horses leave a much cleaner logging site than the usual logging equipment. A horse can drag out logs leaving a trail only as wide as those left by wild game; bulldozers, on the other hand, scar the whole side of the mountain.

John and I decided to take the offer and log out the Priest Camp. We would make a better profit on less work than selling firewood. Firewood required so much handling—cutting it up, loading it by hand onto the truck, unloading and stacking it at our woodyard and then reloading and delivering it to a customer. The horse could pull these larger logs up a ramp onto the logging trailer. The logs would be hauled to the mill and there be unloaded by a forklift.

A week later John began cutting and decking the huge logs. Soon, however, it was evident that our Clydesdale —who had worked so faithfully on the smaller firewood timber—was too small to pull out these huge logs alone.

"We need another horse," John grimly informed me one night. "We just don't have any other choice if we're going to pull the big stuff."

I fought the wave of panic that swept over me. Buying another horse would take the last of our savings and maybe a small loan as well. I saw our savings as my last shred of earthly security—something to fall back on in an emergency. Was this the emergency I'd been dreading?

I was daily sinking further and further under fears that, while I could squelch them, outsmarted me by making me short-tempered with the boys. I nagged John every night with lists of questions: How was the logging going? Did he think things might get better? When? What did he think we ought to do next?

He answered patiently, his lean shoulders bowed under his plaid workshirt and suspenders.

I always kept prying—first the easy questions and then the impossible ones. Finally John would cut me off, exasperated.

"Peggy, I don't know. I can't tell you what's going to happen. If it comes to going broke I'll have to quit and get some other job, okay?" His eyes were hard and his jaw set. "For now, I just have to hang in there and keep doing what I can."

Every night he labored—repairing broken harness or cleaning and filing his chain saw. Periodically the truck brakes went out. Every moment of his evenings and weekends could have been filled with ten different maintenance jobs. And that, on top of his long, exhausting hours in the woods.

Late at night he would apologize for running out of patience. "I know you just need to find out what I'm thinking. I don't know why it makes me so defensive."

"No, I'm the one who's wrong," I'd admit. It was true. Making John worry with me temporarily relieved my ever-present terrors. It made me feel less alone. But adding my fears to his problems never solved anything for very long.

The next afternoon I would have a new supply of anxious questions to unload on John. The cycle would begin again.

John ran an ad in the newspaper, saying he wanted to buy a workhorse. A rancher named Knudson called us about his Percheron.

I left the boys with Bonnie, a good friend and neighbor, and rode with John out to Knudson's ranch. John concentrated on driving, not responding to my attempted conversations. Soon I quit trying and in glum apprehension, watched the scenery going by.

I spotted the gray Percheron before we turned off the highway. His muscular body towered above the other ranch horses grazing there as if he were a mighty giant. I studied the horse with a critical eye while John parked the truck and strode over to shake hands with Knudson.

The horse was at least eighteen-hands high. Our Clyde stood at only sixteen-hands. The Percheron reminded me of an idling locomotive waiting to be given the throttle. Raw power quivered through his gigantic muscles. I started to pray.

"Has he done any logging?" John was asking the crusty cowboy.

"Oh, years ago," Knudson drawled. "I bought him two. . .three years back to use for pulling the hay wagon in the winter. But I only hitched him up a couple of times."

John put a bit into the horse's mouth and shuffled behind him for a brief walk around the pasture. The horse was jittery. Not surprising, since he hadn't been worked in several years. John seemed satisfied with the horse. No one could predict how he would pull when teamed with our Clyde. It was a chance we would have to take. We hadn't heard of any more draft-horse shows and we couldn't afford to go to Idaho, where the Clyde had come from, to buy another horse.

John wrote out a check for the last of our savings and Knudson promised to deliver the horse to the fairgrounds in Helena the following Sunday.

"You . . . you like the horse?" I prodded as we drove

out of the yard.

John shrugged, then smiled at me. "I think I can handle him."

"Oh John, "I thought as I pressed his hand. "How strong and capable you are! How I love your determination and ingenuity."

I wished I could strip away my timidity—that would be real freedom—to have a mind unclouded by the dark net of fear. But I simply couldn't do it.

"Our savings is gone. Our savings is gone," wailed a dirge in my mind. How could I think of anything else?

John cut timber Friday and Saturday and left it where it fell. He needed a team to pull it out. He trucked the Clyde from the mountains to our rented stall at the fairgrounds to have him shod.

Sunday dawned hot and muggy. After church I packed a picnic lunch and we all went to the fairgrounds. The children were eager to see the new horse and visit Clyde. John had harness to repair while we waited for Knudson.

The fairgrounds were teeming. The grandstands at one end were packed with fans who had come to see the horse races. Families with picnic lunches sprawled on blankets, dotting the lawn that stretched over nearly ten acres.

Children shrieked as they climbed on the playground equipment and raced around the baseball diamond. Others darted through the barns and the outdoor stalls at the far end of the park. When we drove up, several children were petting and rubbing our Clydesdale's head as he leaned gratefully over the door of his stall.

Knudson delivered the Percheron and quickly left.

I rolled down the truck windows so that Sam could nap comfortably on the seat; then I walked over to the stalls to watch John work.

The huge Percheron backed away as John approached to harness him.

"He's not used to crowds," John muttered, brushing by me, heading for the truck.

John planned to hook the Percheron to the truck bumper, as Odegaard had done with the Clydesdale, to see how the horse pulled.

The Percheron was jittery about having the truck behind him. But eventually John soothed him enough to back him up to the singletree. John hooked the singletree to the tug lines and straightened the driving reins.

The horse stepped forward at John's "Git up!" But as soon as the big animal felt the weight of the truck on his collar, he backed off and danced sideways.

"Git up!" John ordered firmly again, slapping the beast sharply on the rump with the ends of the drive lines.

This time the horse put his weight into the collar. His hindquarters sank as his mighty thighs pushed into the weight of the load. The truck was moving!

"Whoa!" John grunted when the horse had walked a few paces.

After several more starts and stops pulling the truck, John was satisfied that the horse could be coerced into working for us.

Next, John unhooked the singletree from the bumper, took the reins, and clucked for the horse to walk. John turned the huge gray beast in circles to the right and then the left—stopping the horse and starting him again to see how well he obeyed commands.

"He's got a hard mouth, about like I expected," John informed me as he paced behind the skittery beast. "But he seems to remember commands."

They tramped up and down the alley between the outdoor stalls several more times before John pulled the Percheron to a halt and unhooked the singletree.

"Let's see how he'll like pulling with the Clyde," John suggested with a sly smile.

The boys had lost interest in the horses by this time and had dashed over to the playground equipment.

John dragged out the doubletree. The Percheron tossed his head nervously when our Clydesdale was harnessed with him. As John walked or trotted behind the horses, the Percheron kept rolling his eyes and pulling to the side. His massive weight jerked the Clydesdale sideways and nearly wrenched the smaller horse off his feet.

As the horses rounded the corner of the barn, John was forced to run to keep up with them. I could hear John's low, commanding "Whoa," but only the Clydesdale responded.

When the Clyde tried to stop, the jerk on the lines only made the Percheron more excited.

"Oh, my Lord," I thought, my mouth going dry. "What if John can't hold them?"

John was able to turn the team in a wide circle, but by then both horses were trotting fast. As they broke into a gallop, the reins were ripped out of John's hands, throwing him headlong.

I felt relieved that they hadn't dragged John. But my relief was short-lived. John was on his feet again, shouting as he ran. The horses were galloping around the stables, the doubletree bouncing wildly and slashing at the runaways' hind legs. They were headed straight for the crowded fairgrounds' park a hundred yards away.

My stomach clenched. I couldn't swallow. All those little children! They could never escape those eight gigantic hooves! Even after the horses were out of sight, I could hear the rumbling thunder of their hooves pummeling the ground.

I ran for the truck. My knees buckled unsteadily. I knew I was already too late to head them off.

"Dear God," I sobbed as I fumbled with the keys, "don't let them hurt anybody!"

I gunned the motor and raced around the barns and sheds, hardly daring to think what I might find when I caught up with the horses.

As I rounded the corner of the last barn, I saw them. They were quietly standing and John was unstrapping the harness.

"Is everything all right?" I yelled as I braked the truck in a swirl of dust.

John looked up, flashing his boyish grin.

"Well, these ladies here had quite a scare," he answered quietly, giving me a wink as he led the sweating Percheron back to his stall.

"What happened?" I asked the slim woman who was holding the reins of our Clyde. She was soothing him with little clucking sounds as she stroked his neck.

"Well, she replied, "we were in the barn cleaning out our horses' stalls when we heard a commotion outside. As we ran out of the barn these two runaways nearly plowed over us!"

The shorter woman walked over to us, keeping a wary

eye on the Clyde.

"They were coming right toward us," the second woman added with a shaking voice. "Then, at the last second, the big gray one shied away, pulling this horse down that blind alley. They pulled up short at the wall in the back."

"My Lord," I breathed in amazement. "My wonderful God, You really did protect us!"

John trucked the horses back up to the mountains that very afternoon. I followed with the boys in the car. Although John continued to work the two horses as a team, the hard-mouthed Percheron often caused problems, bolting uncontrollably and lunging with the load rather than pulling evenly.

I was badly shaken and sobered by the thought of what could have happened that afternoon. It was several days before I thought again about whether our house was going to sell before our option on the other house closed. I didn't care one way or the other anymore.

All that really mattered to me now was my family's health and safety. The Lord had dramatically shown me that He was in control. It was much easier to believe now that He would do what was best in the less important financial matters as well.

Chapter 10

Horse and Harness Logging

The sparkling water splashed over smooth golden pebbles in the creek bed. I stuck my toes in and caught my breath at the icy sting of it.

Upstream, Justin and Joey shrieked and called to one another as they splashed in the cold water. Baby Sam napped in his infant seat, shaded by a tall yellow pine.

I lay back on the grassy bank. The smell of pine and sage blanketed me. I marveled at the deep blue Montana sky and the rich contrast it made against the green pines. I snapped off a blade of grass and let the babble of the stream and the aimless drone of a passing bee lull me into an easy, contented peace. The world was so lovely and quiet—for once, everything seemed right.

"Look, Mom," a shadow crossed my face. Joey stood over me and held out his hands. "See the pretty rocks I found? Come and see the dam we're building." he urged me.

We walked a few yards upstream to where he and

Justin had been playing. His chunky hand was soft in mine.

"Someday," I thought to myself, "I'll want to remember how it felt to hold a little boy's hand."

I could hear John walking the horses down the trail. We had come up to the mountain to bring him a picnic supper.

"Hi, guys! Hi, Peg!" he called. The boys barely glanced up, they were so busy constructing their dam.

I ran to put an arm around his waist and walk beside him.

"You tired, Honey?" I asked him.

"Naw—I had a good day. Gee, it's good to see you." He kissed me.

"You boys want a ride?" he called.

"Ya! Ya!" The boys dropped their loads of sand and rocks and came running.

John boosted them up on the Clyde's strong back and led the horses down to the creek for a drink.

The boys giggled and wiggled on the horse's broad back. Their legs stuck out stiffly over the Clyde's belly. They pummeled their dad with questions and John shared his wisdom.

"This a good place to fish, Dad?" Justin asked.

"No. The pool in that oxbow is a good place, though."

"What's a' oxbow, Dad?" Joey inquired, wrinkling his freckled nose.

"An oxbow's a turn in the creek bed, Son—a place where the water turns and tries a new direction."

I sighed contentedly. Our life seemed like water, flowing around an oxbow, being turned by obstacles in our path but led, always, by a mighty Creator who knew our destination. How I wished I could stay here and hold this quiet moment forever.

Our option to buy the new house expired. The owner offered to renew the option for another sixty days.

We declined the offer. The Lord knew, as well as we, that the option ended the fifth of August. He had shown us once He could easily sell our house if He desired. He must want us to stay put. Besides, since our firewood business had never materialized, we no longer needed the country acreage. Our old home on the outskirts of town still suited our needs. The large lot and garage gave John ample room for equipment and supplies.

Only a tiny part of me was sorry to lose that lovely new home. My mind was occupied with other matters now. Since the runaway, my qualms about money had almost disappeared. But new fears had replaced them. I lived in dread of losing John in his very dangerous work.

Many nights he drove into the driveway—late. By the time he arrived I was pacing the floor wondering whether or not I should call my friend Bonnie to watch the boys so that I could go looking for him. Or was I being childishly overanxious? I wrung my hands, while full-color scenes of the most gory accidents danced before my eyes. A chain saw could have ripped off his arm. A tree could have fallen on him. Those two workhorses might have run away and dragged him. Was he pinned under the truck? Had the brakes gone out? I imagined myself trying to drag his mangled body into the car. How could I lift him? Maybe I should ask Bonnie's husband, Chuck, to go with me.

I shook one awful scene from my mind only to have it replaced by a worse one: What if I found him dead?

When John did arrive home, my fears vanished. I rarely mentioned them to him. When I did, he seemed surprised that I had so little confidence in his ability to take care of himself. John felt logging dangerous only to careless people; he was alert and quick on his feet.

The next afternoon when I started preparing supper, the fear nagged me again. What was he doing now? How soon should I expect him home?

He had carefully explained to me every detail of his day. I reviewed them in my mind. John wrapped a chain around each load of logs, then backed the horses up to the logs and hooked the chain to the doubletree. He stood alongside his load, grasped the reins in his hands, and then grunted, "Get up!"

As John drove the horses down the winding mountain trail, he jumped from one side of the load of logs to the other, sometimes riding astride it, always dodging the trees and undergrowth on either side of the trail. The team skidded the logs down the mountain to the loading deck. Then John stopped them, unwrapped the chain, and rode the horses back up the trail for another load.

Sometimes the unruly Percheron would begin to run too fast with a load. John would have to pull the reins around a tree trunk to help him hold the horse. One day as John half-wrapped the reins around a tree, the Percheron lunged away, smashing John's hand into the back side of the tree.

John, never an alarmist, admitted later that he truly believed his hand was going to be broken or ripped off from the weight of that huge horse crushing his hand against the tree. But God was with us again. The hand was sore for only a day or two.

A few days later I peered out from behind the bed sheets whipping on my clothesline to see an old green jeep wagoneer pull up at my front door. Joey and Justin were making mud pies out in the back yard. John had gone to the woods that day with his friend Geno, and, I realized with a start, his friend was sitting in the passenger seat of the wagoneer! A stranger was at the wheel.

My heart stood still. Where was our truck? And where was John?

Then I saw him—slowly sitting up in the back of the wagoneer.

"Why did they bring him here?" I thought numbly, spitting clothespins out of my mouth. "Why didn't they go directly to the hospital emergency room?"

Geno hopped out of the cab and ran to the back to open the doors. To my relief, John jumped up and scrambled out unaided. The two of them talked briefly to the driver who waved good-naturedly and drove off.

"What happened?" I hollered, exasperated that they were acting so casually. "Why were you lying down?"

"Oh, nothing too serious," John laughed, "just catching a quick nap." His smile faded as he came closer and saw my face. "The logging trailer got stuck in the mud in a low spot, and when we tried to push it out with the hitch on the front bumper of the truck, the tongue of the trailer jumped off the hitch and smashed through the truck grill. It rammed a hole in the radiator."

Geno's shoulders shook with laughter. "That old radiator blew up in a cloud of steam!"

John slapped an arm around Geno's shoulders. "Is there some coffee in the house, Peggy? No, I'll fix it," he added as I made a move to go inside.

I returned to the clothesline as the two men jostled each other into the house.

So that was why they had hitched a ride home in the old wagoneer! I was weak with relief; John was all right!

I was slowly learning to trust the timeless truth of Psalm 91, which I prayed over and over again. I memorized verses 10–12: "No harm will befall you, no disaster will come near your tent. For he will command his angels concerning you to guard you in all your ways; they will lift you up in their hands so that you will not strike your foot against a stone."

Now when I was afraid, pacing the floor at night wondering what had happened to make John late, I repeated that promise. It made a gentle, unexplainable peace steal over me.

Chapter 11

My Baby Can't See!

I had stifled my motherly concerns long enough. I was worried about Sam.

Justin had first smiled in the doctor's office when we were waiting for his six-week check-up. The date stuck in my mind. Joey also smiled within two or three days of his six-week birthday. When the first of July rolled around, I began to watch for Sam's first smile.

By the time Sam was eight weeks old, I grew concerned. Not only was Sam not smiling at me, he wasn't even looking at me. Later, I noticed that his eyes wandered a lot, as if he couldn't control them.

In the first week of August, I called Dr. Bennett to ask if Sam ought to be seen right away ... or did some babies just normally take longer to get control of their eye muscles?

"Well, when is baby Sam's next regular checkup?" Dr. Bennett responded briskly.

"Next week. His three-month check-up." I answered.

"We always do a routine check on the eyes at three months," Dr. Bennett attested. "By that age a baby can track a light if you move it back and forth in front of his eyes."

I hung up the phone feeling better. I was grateful that Dr. Bennett was not alarmed.

I mentioned to John a few days later that I hadn't seen Sam smile yet.

"But Dr. Bennett says he'll check Sam's eyes as a matter of routine next week," I added.

"That's good," John replied, glancing sharply at Sam. "Probably good to catch these things early. He may need a little surgery for a weak eye muscle or something, you know."

We were interrupted at that moment by Justin summoning everyone to the bathroom to observe the miracle of the bath water making a whirlpool on its way down the drain.

John left for the woods as usual at 4:00 a.m. on August 16th. I left the two older boys with Mary and sped across town to Dr. Bennett's office for our 10:00 a.m. appointment.

Dr. Bennett listened to Sam's chest for only a few seconds, then abruptly started to leave the room. "I want to check those eyes for you," he said over his shoulder.

In a moment he was back with a tiny flashlight that he swung slowly back and forth in front of Sam's eyes. The baby cooed and gurgled happily, but his eyes continued to dart around the room. They never focused on the light.

"Is there any particular ophthalmologist you prefer?" Dr. Bennett asked matter-of-factly.

"Er . . . Um . . . No." I faltered.

"I'll call and see who can see him now." Dr. Bennett

stated. "You can get the baby dressed."

A cold sweat formed in the palms of my hands. "Now don't go getting nervous," I told myself. I was really glad that we were going to see a specialist right away so that we could get started on the problem.

Outside the heat of August hit me in the face. Sam was fussy as we drove across town. The nurse in the ophthalmologist's office let me feed baby Sam in a little room while we waited for Dr. O'Fallon to see us.

Dr. O'Fallon's exam was slow and methodical. Over and over he studied one of Sam's eyes and then the other.

"Pupil response is good," he stated at last. "Voluntary muscle response is normal."

I began to relax again.

There was a long wait while Sam's eyes were dilated. Then the doctor brought in more instruments with which to look deeper into the eyes.

He searched silently, peering into one eye and then the other. Wasn't he finding anything wrong?

"Lord, enlighten him!" I prayed.

But in a few moments I began wondering if the doctor was stalling for time. Could it be something more than a weak eye muscle?

At last Dr. O'Fallon put down his instruments and picked up Sammy's chart. His eyes never met mine. Instead, he drew tiny circles on the chart as he spoke.

"The optic nerve is dull, not shiny and bright as it should be," he said softly. Kindly.

I felt cold inside. My hands started to shake a little, but I forced myself to think of a sensible question requiring a concrete answer.

"Will he be able to read?"

In response, Dr. O'Fallon began drawing a small diagram on the chart for me.

"The retina is made up of a network of small nerves," he explained patiently. "They branch together, forming larger and larger nerves, until finally at the center of the retina they form the very large optic nerve that connects to the brain. In your son's eyes, he gestured toward Sam, asleep now in my arms, "the small nerves are hardly there at all."

His words came more slowly. He was choosing them carefully. "The optic nerve is very, very small. In *both* eyes."

Dr. O'Fallon paused, then took the plunge. "I don't expect him to have any central vision ... maybe some peripheral vision," he added unconvincingly. "Maybe he will be able to see some shapes and forms."

There were questions then about my pregnancy.

"Anything unusual?"

"No."

"The delivery? Was it normal?"

"Sam was born posterior," I said hollowly.

"That would have nothing to do with eye development." The doctor shook his head.

A mother's optimism dies hard. Stubbornly, I shook myself free of all the confusing questions to look practically to the future.

"Well, what do we do now? Glasses? Is that what he needs?" I asked almost brightly.

Patiently, the doctor repeated what he had already told me, "The baby isn't near-sighted or far-sighted— those things can be corrected with glasses. This condition is not correctable."

I dropped my eyes to my sleeping baby. I could think of no more questions.

Suddenly, I had an impulse to bolt from the room. I yearned to hide my baby. To protect Sammy from the doctor's chilling verdict.

Instead, I stumbled awkwardly to the lobby, my voice breaking as I asked the receptionist for my bill. She looked up and smiled.

"Doctor wants to see that cute little baby again in a month," she chattered cheerfully.

I snatched the invoice from her hand and scooped up my diaper bag. Stumbling to the door, I could feel her bewildered eyes on me. I groped for the door knob and slipped outside.

In the car, huge painful sobs wracked through me. I started the motor, not knowing where to go. Several times I had to pull over to the curb until I could see well enough to drive again.

A dear friend, who already knew about my concern for Sam's eyes, lived nearby. I stopped at her house to cry and to talk until my mind could make some sense out of what I had just learned.

I pushed open her front door.

Judy took one look at my tear-streaked face and held out her arms to me. She was about my age, the mother of two preschoolers. She had been in a wheelchair since she was fifteen; I knew she would understand all the confusion I needed to pour out to her.

Haltingly, I tried to tell her what the doctor had said, but my mind wouldn't work well. All I could remember clearly was that he had said the optic nerve and retina were underdeveloped. Was it something serious? I wasn't sure. I couldn't remember; I didn't think he'd said. Yet somewhere deep inside of me, wrapped in a cocoon, I protected the answer to that question.

On the way home, I repeated over and over again the words of Psalm 91: "No harm will befall you." God *was* with me.

I called Mary, asked her to send the boys home, and busied myself with supper.

At five o'clock John burst through the door. "How was the check-up?" he demanded urgently. "For some reason, I've been wondering about it all day."

I put a finger to my lips and we tiptoed to the bedroom where we could hold one another while I brokenly whispered what I could remember of the doctor's report.

"But what does that mean? What will Sammy be able to see?" John demanded when I had finished.

"I don't know what it means . . . I just don't know," I answered woodenly.

John kissed me distractedly and strode back outside to file his chain saw.

Later that night when Justin and Joey were safely tucked into bed, John leaned his arm on my shoulder as I stood over Sammy's cradle, watching him sleep. I felt the tears welling up again.

"I'm so confused," I sobbed as John held me. The sweet peace had faded away through the evening, and now panic filled the void. "Oh God, please don't let it be serious!"

There seemed nothing else for John and I to say to each other. But his wordless embrace whispered gently: "I'm hurting because of our baby and I'm hurting because you are hurting."

It seemed ironic. Other nights when I was afraid, I had tried to drive away my fear with words—pelting John with questions as if his answers could cement my security back together. But tonight it was his silence that I needed—his arms around me as my mind grappled with Fear itself. I felt his pain, sensed his mind's stunned groping, but stronger than either of these, I felt washed in the strong, surging river of his faith. I hadn't realized before how well I knew John—and there was such comfort in his familiarity!

Late that night, after John had finally fallen asleep flat on his back beside me, my mind searched every corner of Baby Sam's short life. I wanted to uncover new evidence that would prove the doctor wrong.

"What about the times I've seen him lying on a blanket, talking to his little fists as they waved over his head?" I argued with the darkness around me. "What about the way he always seems to stare at the wallpaper beside his dressing table when I'm changing him?"

"He never looked at you, though. He never smiled," came a callous reply from somewhere in the back of my mind.

A mental shutter slammed, stopping the words of the obvious conclusion.

"NO! That's wrong! . . . It can't be true!" I tossed and turned until my tired mind finally closed its arguments, in sleep.

When I awoke, a thick haze of sorrow enveloped me. No rebellion. No anger. Only heavy, aching sorrow.

"Will it be this way every morning as long as I live?" I wondered. "Will every morning seem gray and mournful?"

Holding Sammy was my only comfort ... stroking his soft cheek ... hearing his tiny coos. I rocked him as long as he would let me, studying his precious features.

"My perfect baby," I whispered over and over. "Dear God, he is so beautiful. I won't let them say he isn't perfect!"

My parents lived six hundred miles away. I called them, thinking that sharing the burden with them would lift the heaviness a bit. I was immediately sorry I hadn't waited until I knew more details. I could tell Mom was alarmed about the baby and worried about me. She promised to call back tomorrow and hung up reluctantly.

The boys were outside playing. Sammy was asleep. I knelt down to pray again.

"Jesus, why can't I feel You any more?" I challenged Him. "Please let me feel Your arms around me."

A knock on the front door interrupted me.

A woman from the church stood on the porch, a box of garden vegetables filling her arms. She had attended a women's morning Bible study I had hosted, but I didn't know her well. She was my mother's age.

"Peggy, I just heard about the baby and I came right over," Maxine said quickly when I opened the door.

She dropped the box of vegetables to the porch floor and hugged me tightly while I sobbed on her shoulder.

She sat down beside me on the living room sofa. With her arms clasped around me for almost an hour, she listened. Occasionally Maxine reassured me that she understood my pain.

During our Bible studies I had sensed that she was a

very wise woman, and she still carried that same aura with her. But Maxine did not burden me with her wisdom, only with loving sympathy that was nourishing food to my hungry spirit.

When she left, I knew Jesus Himself had come to my door to weep with me. The burden was lighter. I felt calmer. All the tears had been shed and I could rest.

But even this new peace did not last long. Something was attacking me, trying to break into my mind. I felt like I was standing in the ocean with waves buffeting against me. As each one hit, someone was shouting, screaming in my head, "Your baby is blind! He's blind!"

I staggered against the weight of the wave while it rolled over me.

Then, mercifully distracted by the children or some immediate task of the long afternoon, I could temporarily forget the strange, cruel words. In a few moments the next wave struck, and the ruthless shouting hit my ears. My mind stumbled again with the force of it.

Again the wave passed. I stubbornly forgot the shouting words immediately—as if by refusing to acknowledge the message, the message would never be true.

Late that night I lay in bed, staring at the ceiling. I was too exhausted to sleep or to keep up my fight. The walls of unbelief, which my mind had thrown up so valiantly, were crumbling. Dr. O'Fallon's words fought their way into my memory. Everything he said was coming back to me now.

"I don't expect him to have any central vision.... Maybe he will be able to see some shapes and forms."

"Blind!" I forced myself to whisper the word for the first time.

Suddenly a vision stabbed my mind. I saw myself carrying a heavy cross and following the Lord to Calvary. My cross was easily recognizable. It was the unending agony of watching Sammy through the years ... stumbling when he tried to walk ... confused when other children teased him.

The cross the Lord carried was different; it was my hope. A cruel, ugly thing by the world's standards, but I knew it contained my salvation.

Here, then, was my comfort: trusting that my cross, too, cruel as it seemed, would one day become a victory. Sammy's blindness must be the best thing for Sammy, for John and me, and for the boys—because God had promised to work all things out for the good of those He calls His own (Rom. 8:28).

John was asleep beside me. No matter—my revelation would keep. I snuggled closer to him and immediately slipped into sleep.

Chapter 12

God's Side of the Story

In the morning I didn't mention my vision of the cross to John. Although it continued to comfort me, the ideal it represented seemed too fragile to survive a human conversation. Or could I simply not explain the vision to anyone? Coping with Sam's blindness, like learning to live with dangers of logging, was something John and I had to sort through separately; what worked for me would not work for him. I trusted God would lead John along just as He was leading me.

The vision had begun a change in my way of thinking. As I sprawled on the living room floor doing tummy-exercises, I looked back over my life. Although I had never been conscious of it, I had been protected from pain. Our family had never known much sickness. Injuries happened to other people, but not to us. I saw how blessed we had been. Pain had been all around me, but I had never realized that suffering was a natural, unavoidable part of life.

I saw that God had carefully timed Sam's blindness. My younger self would have fought Him in hot anger. But now, even though I was sobered by my new understanding of reality, this "tragedy" did not change my trust in God's goodness. Evil and suffering entered the world because of Satan's rebellion against God; God was not responsible for Sam's lack of sight.

I was not angry, only saddened, crucified with the agony of a mother's protective love. If only there was something I could do!

My father-in-law, Ed Brooke, precisely expressed my feelings. "I've had my sight for sixty years now," he told me. "If only Sam could take my eyes—I could live my last years without them."

Yet, for all the agony that I was facing—and the agony I saw in Sam's grandparents' eyes and in the eyes of other caring friends—a new freedom bubbled up from within me: a freedom from fear.

What could hurt me further? Another tragedy? It could be dealt with in a similar act of crucified surrender. But it was inconceivable that anything could increase my pain; I could feel nothing more intensely than I felt this anguish.

The next step, after having acknowledged Sam's blindness, was turning to God for healing. Betty and Ted, two friends from our prayer group, stopped over one evening to pray for Sammy. They prayed confidently for Sam's eyes to be completely recreated, for his sight to be made perfect.

"Be healed in the name of Jesus!" Ted closed our little prayer session.

I wanted so badly to believe that Jesus really had

healed Sam at that moment, but to my despair, I couldn't find one feather of faith in my heart.

I didn't trust myself to look at Betty and Ted. Luckily, John was chatting with them; I hoped they wouldn't notice how subdued I was.

I got up from the sofa and took Sam to the privacy of my bedroom to nurse him. He opened his sleepy eyes and looked up at me. My heart stopped. Had his eyes held a steady focus on mine for a moment, or was it only my imagination?

"I think he looked at me!" I almost shouted, but I stopped myself. No, if the Lord chose to heal Sam, He would have to do it without benefit of my declarations. I couldn't risk building myself up with false expectations. I was afraid to hope.

"Lord," I prayed as I rocked Sam in my arms, "I feel so dry inside—as if all my faith is drained out and I have nothing to offer you but emptiness. Oh, Lord, when I meet You alone in prayer, You comfort me with the gentle example of Your cross. But I can't let the comfort I find in those moments lull me into giving up on the resurrection You offer. I must pray for healing—everything in me cries out to You to heal my son! But Faith? I find none, Lord, only a desperate plea for mercy! This then, must be my poor prayer: Heal him, Lord, in spite of me!"

We had not yet told Justin and Joe that Sam was blind.

That night John suggested we tell them. He wanted to protect them from hearing of Sam's blindness through rumors, and I agreed.

The next morning at breakfast, John explained carefully that, although Sammy could see a little, the doctors had told us that he was almost blind. "Of course, we are asking Jesus to heal him," John added.

Justin took the conversation very seriously. "Well, Dad," he asked, "What would it mean if Sam were blind?"

"It would mean he couldn't see, Son," John replied gently.

"I know that," Justin continued in an exasperated tone. "But would it mean that he'd get to have his own dog to help him see?"

John and I stared at each other and then burst out laughing.

"I don't know, Justin," John replied, reaching out and rumpling his tousled blond hair. "Not until he learns to walk anyway."

The boys slid down from their chairs and Justin, his mind probably still on Seeing Eye dogs, caught his elbow on a half-full glass. Milk splattered across the table and onto the floor.

"Run on outside and I'll clean this up," John dismissed the boys.

"It's so good to laugh about Sammy's eyes," John chuckled as he mopped up the floor.

I pushed my chair back and started clearing the table.

"Ya, isn't it great to have children so you don't stay serious about anything too long?" I smiled.

It *was* good to laugh. I realized the answer to my own question of a few mornings ago. No, we wouldn't mourn forever. Somehow we would go on and again find little things to laugh about.

All that day I felt torn between wanting to call out

desperately to God for healing and wanting to rest in tranquil acceptance of living with this sad reality. A battle raged inside of me. But I couldn't put my finger on some deeper issue that needed to be resolved.

The next morning, even before I opened my eyes, I heard myself repeating a prayer that may have gone on all night: "Lord, heal my son!"

John lay awake and praying, too. He reached out and squeezed my hand.

"We need to have faith," I whispered, trying to understand the uneasy feeling prodding me.

John patted my arm.

"We need to have trust," he replied, "that God knows what He is doing."

"But we know that," I mused.

Suddenly I bolted upright. I knew what was bothering me. "John, we don't have expectant faith!"

He turned his head on the pillow to look at me, not sure what I was thinking. John's faith is less complicated than mine; his simple trust stronger.

"Faith is a gift," he said gently.

I wasn't listening. Waves of despair overwhelmed me as I realized how weak my faith really was.

"We're Sam's parents, John! What if he's blind all his life because we haven't the gumption to stand up and 'claim' the Bible promises for his healing?" I burst into tears.

John contemplated a moment and then said softly, "Maybe it's true we ought to 'stand on faith' on the Bible promises. Betty and Ted are 'standing on faith' right now that Sammy is healed. But—maybe because of the way God has shown us that nothing can happen to us that is out of His control—well, we know God could have any number of ideas in mind for Sam. We know we can trust God to bring about the greatest good through this seemingly tragic situation."

I sank back on the pillow and nodded slowly.

"Yes, God can heal Sammy, Hon," John continued softly. "But His doing it doesn't depend on our following the right formulas. You can't take the responsibility for Sam's blindness. Faith is a gift from God, a gift of mercy . . . and so is healing. He has given us whatever faith we have . . . and no matter how small it is, we can trust it is enough. Because from the bottom of our hearts we trust *Him*."

Now I knew what had been pestering me since yesterday. John's simple faith had easily penetrated to the heart of the matter—I was grappling with Satan's accusations of guilt!

A *new* freedom surged through me. John grabbed both my hands for a quick prayer before Justin and Joey, pattering in pajama feet, reached our bedroom door.

"Lord, we trust you. Please Lord, heal our son," John prayed.

I echoed his prayer, no longer in desperation, but in trust.

As I bathed Sam that day, or dressed him, or nursed him, I offered praise to God. I knew that God is pleased with the praise of His people—that our praise is the key to entering His presence (Ps. 100:4). I resolved to saturate Sam in my songs of praise, thereby saturating him in God's presence.

The fifth morning after the visit to the doctor, I woke up, exhilarated! God had given me a dream that led me out of the valley to the mountaintop! I opened my eyes from a new perspective. At last, I saw the blindness as part of Sammy, not some separate enemy to be defeated!

I remembered my dream: I saw the Lord at the time of Sam's conception. In His hand He held a tiny baby—blond, blue eyed, and blind. Searching the earth for a suitable home, He cradled the child, as if reluctant to impart so precious a gift on His thankless people.

He paused for a moment over the drafty apartment of an unwed mother. My son could have been born there, possibly unwanted and unadoptable because of his eyes.

But His mighty glance swept on—past the hovel of a drunkard and pausing over the home of a wealthy man.

In a moment the almighty One shook His head. No, He knew the man too well. He was an impatient father. Perhaps, he would even be ashamed of a blind child.

At last the Lord turned and caught sight of our old brick house. His brow furrowed as He pondered. Then He bent and tenderly placed the precious gift in our care.

Why He chose us to receive Sam, and the entourage of graces that accompanied this special child, was not revealed to me.

Humbled with gratitude, I could now weep with joy! The dark hours of confusion, rebellion and guilt were gone.

And seeing the blindness in this new way—as really part of Sam—I found myself unspeakably grateful that this special baby was safely in my care and not somewhere else!

The sunshine was back. And I now viewed the world with a heart bursting with joy!

How far I had come in learning what really mattered in life—in learning how it felt to be free from so many fears. But God was not satisfied with me, yet. In a short while He would begin to dig even deeper—past the fear —to some deep seated anger I didn't even know I was hiding.

Chapter 13

Reaching for Hope,
Wrestling with Hurt

"Watch, Mom! Watch me!" Justin pleaded from his bedroom.

I set the candy jar down on the coffee table and sprinted, dust cloth in hand, to the door of his room.

Justin was squatting in the middle of his carpeted bedroom floor. It was a pleasant enough room, although crowded. I had wallpapered the old plaster walls in a yellow and white stripe. Justin and Joey's white, painted bunk beds occupied one wall with Sam's crib crowded against the adjoining wall.

The tip of Justin's pink tongue protruded out the corner of his mouth. His brow was furrowed in deep concentration. Slowly and painstakingly he was tying his shoes.

"That's great, Honey!" I raved as he finished and beamed triumphantly up at me.

"See how good I can do it?" he pointed out proudly. "Now can you teach me to read?"

I laughed and set down my dust cloth as he ran to find a story book. I didn't mind the interruption. Kindergarten started next week, and Justin was more than eager to learn. We could both use a restful story time.

We had all been up late last night. John and I had taken Sam to our prayer group meeting. We wanted the "healing ministers" of our group to lay hands on Sam and pray for his healing. That way we would have fulfilled James 5:14-15: "Is any of you sick? He should call the elders of the church to pray over him and anoint him with oil in the name of the Lord. And the prayer offered in faith will make the sick person well; the Lord will raise him up."

We arrived late, as usual, and sat in the front row—in the only available chairs. Our prayer group met in the basement of the famous old cathedral of St. Helena. The semi-circle of nearly two hundred folding chairs crowded the room. As John hurried us up the crooked path between chairs, I noticed Joey limping.

"Oh great." I thought grimly, my motherly halo slipping several notches. He only had one shoe on! I remembered: At suppertime he had told me he couldn't find his shoe. I had assured him I would help look for it after we ate. But, of course, in the hustle to get supper dishes done and children, toys, and security blankets in the car, I never thought of the shoe again.

"Well, be grateful it's summertime," I silently tried to cheer myself. But I was crimson down to my collarbone and sticky with sweat below that.

After the regular prayer meeting, a large circle of friends and community elders gathered around to pray for Sam. I don't remember all the words that were said that night, but I do remember one woman in particular who laid her hands gently on sleeping Sam and prayed that his healing would be a day-by-day improvement which we could see and rejoice in. Another young man reached out to lightly touch Sam's eyes and prayed, "Lord Jesus, give this baby Your eyes to see with."

Like Jesus' mother, I pondered these words for my child in my heart. I was grateful for the support of the many people who loved and cared for us. Friends and relatives from all over the country had been calling or writing to say they and their friends were praying—people who wouldn't ordinarily feel comfortable talking about prayer.

I came home that Tuesday night tired, but hopeful. Exhausted as he was, John went outside to work on his truck brakes. It was after ten o'clock. I hustled the boys into pajamas as fast as I could, ignoring the toothbrush ritual.

Now, in the routine of the next afternoon's house-work, my enthusiastic hope sagged.

The phone rang just as Justin and I finished our story book. It was Judy, my friend in the wheelchair. She was calling to pray with me. We had resolved to call each other daily to pray together for Sam's healing and for hers. Having a prayer partner increased my confidence in prayer—and was a good reminder to both Judy and me that persistence in prayer was too important to be for-gotten in the midst of our busy daily routines.

Every prayer time with Judy was reaffirmation for me of the trust I felt in the goodness of God. When we prayed, we concentrated on praising God for His kind-ness and mercy, rather than on the mountain that needed to be moved. Our trust was growing. Ours was a God who desired healing and wholeness for His children.

I propped up Sam in his wind-up swing in the kitchen while I prayed with Judy. He was protesting loudly by the time I hung up the phone.

Justin, who had heard Sam crying from the other room, came running with a little pink plastic rabbit. He set it on the tray that formed the front piece of Sam's swing seat.

Immediately, Sam's howling stopped. In jerky, un-coordinated movements, he maneuvered his three-month-old fists to grasp the rabbit clumsily by the ears. He stuffed them into his mouth and gummed them with slobbering content.

"Jesus, do I dare believe what I'm seeing?" I gasped in my mind. I was like a child needing reassurance from a parent.

"He saw the rabbit, Mom," Justin said softly, looking up for my reaction.

"Yes, Sweetheart," I answered quietly, wracking my brain to think of what other sense the baby could have used to find the rabbit. I was sure the toy had made no noise when Justin placed it in the tray. Maybe it was only coincidence that Sam had stopped crying at that very moment. Sam's hand movements were so uncoor-dinated, he may not have intentionally reached for the toy rabbit at all!

Justin was already pulling the little rabbit out of Sam's grip and hiding it behind his own back, giggling. "Look, Sammy, see the rabbit?" he taunted merrily, dangling the little toy in front of Sam's face again.

Sammy gurgled in response. His eyes darted about,

uncontrolled.

Justin's voice seemed to excite Sammy, but the baby was not making any attempt to reach for the rabbit. For a few moments more, Justin played with the baby. Then Justin lost interest, dropped the rabbit back on the tray in front of Sam, and ran off to play.

Again Sam's chubby hands moved unsteadily toward the rabbit. He grasped the toy and fumbled with it until he got it into his mouth.

I pulled the rabbit away gently and silently placed the rabbit on the tray again. This time Sam paid no attention to it. Instead he started to squirm and fuss to get out of the swing.

I tried not to hope. But I couldn't entirely squelch a small, bubbly feeling in my heart. As the day wore on, however, I was less and less sure that anything important had taken place.

Meanwhile, John's large timber sale at Priest Camp was coming to an end. There were no more timber sales being put up for bids that fall, so John signed up with the Teamsters' Union. He hoped to get a job working on construction at least until the snow flew.

One afternoon the call came.

"This is Don with the Teamsters' Union," the man said. "We have a job for John driving a pilot car up on McDonald Pass if he can be there by 5:00 p.m."

I glanced at the clock. It was three o'clock now and John was at Priest Camp, an hour's drive away. McDonald Pass was another hour's drive, or even more, from there.

"If he wants the job, have him call me back by four," the union man continued brusquely before he hung up the phone.

"Heavens, how will John ever get to a phone on time?" I wondered. Should I jump in the car and go barreling out to the mountains? Or should I be sensible?

But the Priest Camp logging operation would end in a day or two and John did need more work. John had been waiting for a chance to get a Teamster job and I knew it would be a long time before John's name again moved to the top of the union list. I might as well try.

I snatched Sammy out of bed and ordered Justin and Joe to jump in the car.

I grabbed some graham crackers out of the cupboard and filled a thermos with water to take with me. Juggling Baby Sam, the package of crackers, the thermos, some diapers, baby clothes, Joey's security blanket, and the car keys, I made my way out the door.

I drove our little Subaru wagon as fast as I dared. The summer heat blew through the open windows. The road wound leisurely through the grass-and-sage-covered foothills of the Helena Valley.

But when I turned off the pavement and started up the steep, winding gravel road that would take us the last ten miles, I knew I couldn't risk speeding. The gravel was loose, the corners sharp. I rolled up the car windows to keep out the dust and ordered Justin to do the same in the back seat.

All the while I was singing nursery rhymes to keep the boys' spirits up. Occasionally we passed crackers. In my mind I pleaded with Jesus that John would be done for the day and that he would already have the horses in the corral when we arrived. I knew that unharnessing the horses and putting away equipment would require another half hour of his precious time.

It was four o'clock when I braked in a swirl of dust at the gate of Priest Camp. Miraculously, my prayers were mostly answered. John was already leading the unharnessed horses to the corral. He looked up in alarm at the sound of the car.

"What's wrong?" he shouted as I pushed open the door.

"It's a Teamsters' job!" I yelled "They called at three. They want you to call back by four and be up to McDonald Pass by five."

John whistled to the horses. He hustled them the rest of the way up the trail to the pole corral. It was hidden by the tall pines, but I could imagine him tossing a bale of hay in behind the horses and whipping a skillful knot with bailing twine to secure the rails.

In a few minutes John trotted back down the trail. Then, waving me out of the way, he started the truck and backed it around with a roar.

"Honey, it might already be too late! And what will you do about supper?" I yelled after him.

"Just follow me down and I'll stop at ranches along the way and try to call him," John shouted back as his tires spun in the dirt and the truck swerved away.

I trailed him at a slower pace. I was tired and let down. My delight in our perfect timing of arriving just as John was done for the day dried up like morning's dew in the heat of the sun. John hadn't even thanked me—to say nothing of greeting me or the boys. I was unreasonably disappointed that John expected me to trail him right back down the mountain when the boys hadn't even had time to play in the creek. They had been so good on the ride up—now we were just turning around and starting our hot drive all over again!

If I had not been so engulfed in self-pity, I would have realized I was blaming John for things over which he had no control—my tiredness, for instance. Instead, I asked myself if John ever thought about how easy being a man was. Why, when he wanted to go somewhere in a hurry, he jumped in the truck and went! No diapers to change, no whining to endure!

"What is he planning to do about supper?" I thought grumpily.

I could see the dust flying from behind John's truck. The tall pines lining the winding road made it impossible to tell how far ahead of me he was. I resented his reckless speed. I had the safety of the boys to think of.

Twice John stopped at ranch houses then jumped into the truck and careened off down the road just as I came in sight of him. He was knocking on the door of the third ranch house when I passed him. Would he find anyone at home? At the moment I didn't care.

I drove down to the end of the gravel road and braked to a stop outside of the little country store at Canyon Creek. It would be fun to buy something cool for the boys to sip. Justin and Joey whooped and scrambled out of the car.

Where he had lain against the plastic car seat, Sammy's little body was hot and dripping wet. I changed his diaper quickly then followed the boys into the dim coolness of the old store.

We explored the narrow aisles piled high with brightly packaged convenience and "junk" foods. The worn wooden floors dipped gently toward the collection of cubby holes forming the Canyon Creek Post Office at the back of the store. We selected Popsicles from a wheezing cooler and stepped back out into the dry heat.

As we came out on the wooden walkway in front of the store, John was just turning into the gravel drive.

Slamming on the truck brakes, he grabbed his coat and hopped out. He jumped into our car and rolled down the window to call across the driveway. "Peg, I got ahold of him and I got the job! I'm going to take the car and cut across on Birdseye Road. I'll get there late, but the guy driving the pilot car now will just have to keep driving till I get there. Can you bring supper out to me?" He didn't wait for an answer, but waved broadly as he roared away down the highway in the Subaru.

I sighed, not even feeling gracious enough to be grateful that he had gotten the job. I boosted the boys up on the truck seat and observed testily that I might as well take my time. Poor me! It seemed apropos that I had been abandoned with three children in the middle of nowhere.

Sammy was crying and I nursed him behind the wheel of the dusty truck. When he was finished, I shoved John's lunch pail, a coil of rope, some chain, and a rain slicker off the seat to make room for the boys. Their legs were short; they wouldn't mind the clutter on the floor. I turned the key and let the protesting motor idle its way back out to the highway.

Later that evening I borrowed Geno and Patti's car, rather than wrestle with our old truck, and packed John's supper and the three boys into it. I headed for McDonald Pass, fifteen miles west of Helena.

The union construction crew was paving a new section

of highway on the pass. John's job was to drive back and forth piloting traffic through the single lane of highway that was ready for use. It was a dull assignment at best, and I wondered how John would stay awake until his shift ended at 1:00 a.m.

I pulled to the side of the road, waiting with the stopped traffic, for John to come back in the pilot car. The boys were tired of the insides of cars. Out they scrambled to climb around on the steep rocky hillside that rose sharply from the side of the road. They were dressed in patched play clothes, dirty and rumpled from the day's adventures. We had forgotten a belt for Joey, and now, as he scrambled around on the rocks and slid down the loose dirt to the roadway, his pants kept slipping down to his knees.

"What's taking John so long?" I muttered to myself.

It was really embarrassing, sitting there with my boys looking like hillbillies. Sammy was growing fussy. John's supper was in a tired-looking brown paper bag that I would have to deliver to him by jumping over the rocks and past the impatiently waiting line of cars.

"This is the life, all right!" I grumbled bitterly as I cruised back down the mountain to Helena a half-hour later.

I had finally given up the idea of seeing John and left his supper with a red-headed flag lady. The boys were asleep in an exhausted heap in the back seat. But I was in no mood even to savor the peace and quiet. I wondered if John would ever be ready to go back to work at the bank. What was it I had resolved long before—about never letting a wall of resentment build between us? It was easier to grumble a list of reasons why I was right and he was wrong than examine what was really making me so angry.

I would wait and deal with my anger some other day.

Chapter 14

Seeing with Jesus' Eyes

The next morning I crept out of bed at seven, when the boys woke up. I had to straighten up the house for a visitor. In response to my letter to a school for the blind, asking for information on raising Sam, a man named Paul Clancey was dropping by.

He was a tall, plain looking man with thick glasses. I liked him immediately. Not only did he care enough about blind children to work at the school, he and his wife had adopted a blind baby girl.

Mr. Clancey told me about the school and about the state and national facilities available to Sam. But his first interest seemed to be me and my reaction to Sam's condition.

"How have you and your husband adjusted to the idea of Sam's blindness?" he asked me, his kind eyes studying my face.

I told him of our trust in the goodness and provision of God and of my overwhelming gratefulness that Sam was mine to love and care for.

Mr. Clancey seemed moved and even impressed that we were so quickly able to cope with the situation.

"It's God, you know," I told him again. "I think He carefully prepared us for this all our lives."

I didn't share my dream with him; I wasn't sure that Mr. Clancey would believe that God, in love, had revealed to me His process of selecting Sam's parents.

Sam woke up from his nap shortly after Paul Clancey arrived. Paul played with Sam briefly before handing him back to me. I cuddled Sam, wondering self-consciously if a professional like Mr. Clancey was noticing things I was doing wrong with my baby.

Paul briefly explained the content of some books he would leave with me.

"You know," Paul observed after a few moments, "I've been watching Sam very closely while you were holding him. He certainly holds his head up well. He must be seeing a lot of light!"

"Do you really think so?" I probed eagerly.

I had already explained as accurately as I could Dr. O'Fallon's diagnosis.

"Oh yes. A blind child is very slow to learn to lift his head because, of course, he sees nothing. Another thing I've noticed—Sam is really affectionate and cuddly with you. That's a very good sign! A child missing any one of the five senses will often seem unaffectionate because he doesn't as easily sense your affection for him."

I could have kissed Mr. Clancey's feet. Here was a knowledgeable professional who spoke nothing but positive, glowing words and encouragement. He was even saying that Sam seemed ahead of most blind children his age!

How glad I was that, ever since his birth, I had "spoiled" Sam by taking him to bed with me to nurse. That was the privilege of a third-time mother, I had rationalized—to scrap all the rules about baby discipline and cuddle him as often as I could. Looking back, I realized I had unknowingly showered him with warmth and security in what must have been a world that was otherwise dark.

After Mr. Clancey's visit, John and I devoured the books he'd left. They were filled with positive and supportive advice about the challenge of raising a blind child. I felt eager to begin Sam's training. Mr. Clancey's words—about how well Sam held up his head and about how affectionate he was—sang in my mind for the next week.

Once, twice, Sam again seemed to reach for toys. When he was picked up by a stranger at our prayer meeting, he stiffened and pulled his head back as if he were looking at the woman's face. Suddenly, he burst into tears.

But these scattered incidents could easily have been exaggerated by my imagination. Sam's eyes still wandered; I dared not let myself hope too much.

Even though I believed I had completely accepted Sam's blindness, moments when the somber reality of just what blindness could mean crashed down on me.

A week or so after Mr. Clancey's first visit I drove the car home in the midst of noon-hour traffic. I was calculating how long it would take me to whip together a lunch for Justin, flush it down him, and whisk him and the other two boys back into the car for the short drive to school. Suddenly, out of the corner of my eye, I saw a bright flash of color. It may have been a car in the other lane of traffic—or maybe a fluttering flag at a used car lot. At any rate, my mind seemed to spit out like a computer the words the ophthalmologist had used: peripheral vision.

The thought distracted me so that I almost plowed into the car ahead of me, stopped at a red light. "That's peripheral vision!" my mind shouted. "Just a bright flash of color that is gone before you recognize it."

"I don't expect him to have any central vision . . . maybe some peripheral vision." The doctor's words echoed through my mind.

Tears clouded my sight as the impact of what he had tried to tell me sank in. It didn't matter that Sam held his head up and saw a lot of light. What good was light if it was blurry and fuzzy, revealing only hazy forms? What good were all these books about stimulating a child to use his sight when all he would see would be an improved blur?

In that clear flash of insight, I also saw myself as a product of the age of scientific reasoning. Even though I had accepted Sam's blindness, I matter-of-factly assumed that doctors and other professionals, such as Mr. Clancey, would do something to enable Sam to lead a normal life. I knew I must face the harsh possibility that nobody —except, of course, God, the Miracle Worker—could do anything.

By this time it was mid-September, nearly time for our next scheduled visit with the ophthalmologist. I had made two appointments, only a day apart. One with Dr. O'Fallon and the other with a second specialist. I wanted to hear more than one doctor's opinion.

This time John went with me. Dr. O'Fallon again carefully explained to John and me that the optic nerve and retina were very underdeveloped—probably even dead. There was nothing he could do for Sam.

The second doctor, Dr. Porini, agreed with Dr. O'Fallon's diagnosis. But Dr. Porini recommended that we go to the University Hospital in Salt Lake City for further tests. On his chart, which I did not see until several months later, the doctor wrote: "I am sending these parents to the university doctors because what I have seen is too devastating a report to give to the parents myself."

John and I were delighted to have the opportunity to do something for Sam. We left Dr. Porini's office feeling satisfied. We had an appointment in Salt Lake for the following month.

In October, when Sam was five months old and crawling all over the house, a second representative from the school for the blind came to see me. Sam was napping when he arrived.

Mr. Paulson, who was to become our regular representative from the school, urged that I not give in to my overly protective motherly instincts.

"Blind children learn to crawl very slowly," he told me, "so you must constantly stimulate his movement with noisy or musical toys. When Sam does start to crawl about, you may want to protect his head with a helmet. Otherwise, he may constantly bang into things and bruise himself. But he will learn to be independent much more readily if you resist the urge to overprotect him."

"Why, Sam is crawling already," I exclaimed, "and I

can't recall him ever bumping his head. He goes through doorways and all over the house."

Mr. Paulson was so surprised that he wanted to see this for himself. When Sam awoke, I changed him and put him down on the floor. Sam not only crawled, but seemed to be showing off. With much wiggling and grunting he crawled through a complicated maze formed by the piano bench and the columnar legs of the piano. But he never bumped a thing.

"That baby has got to be seeing very well!" Mr. Paulson asserted with a shake of his head.

A week later at the University Hospital in Salt Lake, a young resident doctor and then a renowned retina specialist checked Sam for about thirty minutes, using various lenses. Finally, the specialist called John and I into his office and cleared his throat.

"Well," he said, "this is most unusual."

The doctor held up a large chart of the eye for us to see and pointed to the retina which formed the back of the eyeball. "Now, these blood vessels and nerves that make up the retina have a certain pigmentation, or color, to them, just like your skin," he told us. "Your son has a condition called 'ocular albinism.' That means there is no pigmentation on the retina of his eye. You know what an albino is?" the doctor continued.

We both nodded slowly.

"Well, your son has a retina like that of an albino. But the peculiar thing is that he exhibits no other albino characteristics. You see, you could have a little patch of skin somewhere on your body with no pigmentation, and it wouldn't cause you much trouble. But why that patch should happen to be on the retina—and then why it should happen to be on *both* retinas—well, it's just very unusual."

"But what about the optic nerve?" I broke in.

"Oh, it seems normal," he answered off-handedly.

"*Normal?* Did you say the optic nerve looks normal?" I almost shouted.

"M-m-m . . . yes, that's what I would say," the specialist assured me.

"Well, what do you think he will be able to see?" John prodded eagerly.

The doctor was very wise. "I don't know what he will be able to see. You, the parents, can already tell me more about what he can and can't see than I can tell you. It's bound to affect his sight, not having either retina normal. But I just couldn't venture a guess as to how much he will be able to see."

A quiet delight was bubbling through me. The optic nerve is normal! God was healing Sammy one day at a time. And for the first time I not only dared to believe it, but my whole being knew it was true!

Here was a renowned specialist expressing confidence in my ability to observe rationally what Sammy was seeing and not seeing! I felt like a captive bird set free to fly to the sun. I dared to believe at last Sammy's eyes were being restored by God. Day by day I could rejoice and watch it happen.

John smiled at my new-found joy. He had never doubted God would heal our baby.

Back in Helena, I immediately took Sam to Dr. O'Fallon; I wanted my miracle confirmed. I couldn't wait for him to look into Sam's eyes and see the "normal" optic nerve where before there had been only a "dead" one.

But to my disappointment, the doctor didn't show amazement at all. Instead, he looked up at me with a blank stare that made me feel guilty for interrupting his hectic schedule.

"Everything looks the same," the doctor said quietly.

"You mean...you mean the optic nerve hasn't changed?" I stammered.

"Lord," I prayed, "this is really embarrassing."

"It still looks very small to me," he stated flatly. Then he flipped on his little flashlight—as if to give himself something to do—and swung it back and forth in front of Sam.

"Jesus," I thought, piqued at myself and exasperated with God, "now this poor doctor thinks I'm trying to embarrass him or something by rushing in here with a conflicting report from the Big Wheels in Salt Lake."

"And he's how old? Five months? And still not able to focus on this light?" the doctor sighed, snapping off the light.

He made a movement to gather up Sam's charts; but, instead, his eyes shot back, startled, to Sam. For just as the doctor had turned off the light, Sam had reached out two baby fists and plucked the flashlight from the doctor's fingers.

But the doctor, puzzled, only grunted and excused himself as he hurried from the room.

I sat for a few moments, motionless, pondering the meaning of all that was happening. The incident in Luke 17:11–19 floated into my mind. Jesus had healed ten lepers. But not immediately. Rather, He healed them after they had left Him, while they were "on the road," as if to allow them the freedom to choose their response to

Him.

They could have looked at their healing and said, "Well, isn't that a coincidence? Shortly after that guy prayed for me I got well." Or, "Well, you know, I never really was very sick any way."

Apparently only one leper gave credit to Jesus for healing him.

What was I to learn about this God of mine whose miracles were so subtle they allowed scoffers to go on scorning? What was He trying to teach me about faith in Him that He preferred not to confirm positively with Dr. O'Fallon's prognosis? Jesus could open the eyes of the blind. Did He wish the eyes of faith to see miracles that others would never see?

"Lord Jesus, give this baby Your eyes to see with," a young man had prayed over Sammy. Perhaps that prayer held a clue to the answers to my questions.

Chapter 15

Snow on My Fire

John's job, driving pilot car, lasted only three days. We were both relieved to have it over with. He was now eligible for the union's "B" list and would, we hoped, be called for better jobs.

After counting up our slim profits from logging, we decided to sell the horses.

Although John had loved working with the horses, he could see that the method was too slow and unwieldly to be profitable. The work was so hard that he doubted he could keep up the pace as he grew older. For John horse logging had been a wonderful dream fulfilled. "Something to tell my grandkids about," he called it, but it was not something that would sustain our family much longer.

John took a job as a timber faller about fifty miles from our home, in the mountains. He left for work by four-thirty or five every morning.

That winter was one of the longest and fiercest in Helena's history. The first snow fell early in November and stayed on the ground until spring. Temperatures dropped to below zero and remained there. The warm chinook winds, which ordinarily blew in several times during the cold months, bringing spring-like weather that melted the snow, never arrived.

John was always exhausted. While I still slept, John rolled out of bed and dressed in layers: three or four sweaters and two pairs of long johns under his pants. Over these he added wool snow pants and a waterproof coat. Then he loaded the truck with his lunch bucket which I had packed the night before, two chain saws and files, gasoline and oil cans, tools, and spare chain saw parts. He wore a hard hat and a logger's tape measure, a marking crayon, a small tree counter, and spiked boots for walking on the fallen trees in order to cut off the limbs. All day he tramped knee-deep through the snow, logging his thirty-pound chain saw.

John sized up each tree, calculating exactly how to make it fall where he wanted. He made a notch about a quarter of the way through the tree on the side he intended it to fall. Next, he would "back cut" the opposite side of the tree until the cut approached the first notch. If the tree did not begin leaning into the notch from its own weight, John set a plastic "falling wedge" into the crack of the back cut, driving the wedge in with two or three good whacks of his axe head. He continued cutting toward the notch, always watching for the first movement of the tree. As it began to fall, John moved also, plowing as rapidly as he could, through the snow at a 135 degree angle from where the tree would land.

With a gigantic CR...ACK! the tree broke through the remaining "hinge" of wood and thundered toward the ground. On impact, the powdery snow bellowed high into the air, creating a blinding miniature snow-storm. The tree and logger were blanketed as the snow floated back down.

Next John squared up the butt end of the tree. Then he shoved the nail attached to the end of his tape measure into the butt and walked the length of the tree, cutting limbs as he went. When the tree had been cut into the correct sawmill lengths, he was ready to wade through the snow to his next tree.

By three or four in the afternoon, John began the hour-long drive home. The heat of the truck melted the snow on his frozen clothes. His body, which had been hot all day from continual exercise, cooled down and chilled from the sweat and melting snow on his clothing.

John arrived home shivering. Quickly stripping off his wet clothes and hanging them to dry on chairs and counter tops in the kitchen, he huddled against our wood-burning stove.

Later, after changing into dry clothes, and eating supper, John spent what was left of the evening filing his chains to a precise angle and cleaning and repairing the saws. By nine o'clock John collapsed into bed, falling instantly into a deep sleep.

The winter rekindled old frustrations for me. I yearned for a more leisurely life. Therapeutic chats over tea with friends like Geno's wife, Patti, soothed my flagging morale.

"What's on your menu tonight?" I asked Patti one afternoon. We were relaxing beside my warm kitchen fire, our feet propped up on chairs for footstools. We cradled our teacups in our hands, sipping the hot brew occasionally. The voices of her three children and mine drifted out to us from the children's bedroom where the toys were stored.

Patti shrugged.

"Spaghetti, I suppose," she said. Patti's Italian spaghetti was delicious. "I don't know what we'd eat at my house without spaghetti."

"Or Campbell's soup," I laughed. Hamburger casseroles were the mainstay at my table.

"It's funny what one remembers from childhood," I mused as Sammy crawled out to the kitchen. Patti picked him up and bounced him on her lap. "My father said once that if times ever got tough a person could always survive if he had a crop of potatoes stored in his basement. I suppose he was reflecting his Irish heritage. But you know, I haven't been worried about grocery prices going up this year because when I go to the store I always have in the back of my mind the picture of those two hundred pound bags of potatoes we have in the basement." We had bought them in the fall from a nearby potato farmer.

Patti chuckled. "That's probably how Geno feels about spaghetti," she said. "What makes me feel good is fresh fruit and vegetables. As long as I can afford that kind of food I feel ... well, like a good mother. If my children are snacking on a carrot or apple I feel successful."

"The ideal Mother, free from guilt about cavities or malnutrition." I teased. "I do the same thing, and when I bake bread, especially whole wheat, I feel like old Mother Earth or something."

Patti nodded.

"It's funny," I continued, "it doesn't matter how

strained our budget is, there is always enough. Isn't God amazing?" I was thinking again how glad I was that our home had not sold the summer before. How would we ever have managed the large house payments on the new home? As always, God knew what He was doing; our disappointments were a blessing in disguise.

"Yeah," Patti leaned forward in her chair, her hazel eyes ablaze, "and God always keeps us guessing because all the things we plan get messed up. But everything we need—it's there!" Patti always talked as if she could read my thoughts.

"We've cut back on desserts," I told her, "like ice cream—we only have it on Sunday now. During the week it's a piece of fruit or even bread and jam. But you know, it's been good for the kids. They look forward to it so much. It makes Sunday—the whole day—taste good. Eating it has become a special Sunday tradition. I like to see the boys savor it. My mom and dad used to talk about ice cream being such a rare and special treat when they were kids. They had it maybe three times a summer. I like to think my boys are having the same experience."

Sam was fussy now and I took him from Patti to nurse him.

"Good little baby," she whispered, giving him one last pat. "He seems to see so well now, doesn't he, Peggy?"

"Oh, yes," I agreed. "He's crawling at least four feet —maybe more like five—to reach for toys he wants. I keep testing him—over and over just to be sure. It's wonderful to watch! The new ophthalmologist, the people from the school—everyone just watches Sam in amazement!"

"Oh, Peggy, I'm so glad," Patti said almost prayerfully.

"You know, Patti," I said softly, brushing Sammy's soft cheek as he nursed eagerly, "I am so grateful for the miracle Sammy is. We are so blessed. So fortunate! And yet, you know what disgusts me about myself? I don't keep gratitude in the forefront of my thoughts. Even with this miracle baby to be thankful for, little things frustrate me so easily."

Patti closed her eyes and sighed, nodding in understanding.

"I can't help it. Not getting ahead financially is beginning to drive me crazy. Sure God has always provided, and I'm not frightened about money any more, but . . . it doesn't seem fair.

"John is doing what he wants to do. So when do I get the nice things I want? I'd like to know that I can occasionally eat out at an expensive restaurant. That someday I'll have a new house."

"Is your house getting to you again?" Patti sympathized.

I sighed. Our old house exasperated me. Although John and I had remodeled a great deal, my eyes always wandered to what remained undone.

Our old, secondhand furniture looked shabby. Our kitchen, with its single white porcelain sink and white metal cabinets, was old-fashioned; the dirt-floor basement stood useless except for storage; the second story remained unfinished except for one bedroom.

"You know, Patti," I confessed unhappily, "sometimes I think that it isn't the things I need; it's the hope that I need . . . the anticipation . . . the dream that someday those things will be mine. That's why I need a savings account, I guess. So that I can persuade myself that someday everything I want will be mine. That's what frustrates me now . . . I can't see a better future coming."

"It doesn't bother John at all, does it?" Patti asked. "Not having all those things someday."

"He doesn't understand," I stated quietly.

I knew it wasn't a fair statement. John was always understanding, always ready to listen. But something inside me blamed John for my unhappiness more and more. After all, he had imposed this new lifestyle on me! Why had I never noticed before how different we were? I recalled the first year we had lived in our old house. We had cooked on and heated with an old wood-burning stove. John had been delighted with the notion of "pioneering." The old stove had annoyed me. It burned my bread on one side and left it under-baked on the other. Tending the fire tied me down. Roasts or baked goods that required a long oven time could never be left alone. As for convenience foods, none of them would bake properly with the imprecise temperatures of the oven. Even simple box cakes came out scorched on the outside and oozy as pudding in the middle.

Eventually I did begin to take pride in my skill at baking with a wood fire, but, thank goodness, John suggested we move my electric stove into the kitchen the next winter. He built a separate wood stove for heat.

"I guess I might as well admit I'm ready for John to quit this wild goose chase and go back to the bank," I told Patti as she called her children to put on coats and boots.

She smiled her quiet sympathy.

That night a glimmer of hope that John was changing his mind seeped into my heart.

"I never want to go through another winter like this," John stated quietly as he pushed his plate back with his elbows and rested his head in his hands.

I was taken by surprise, but quickly recovered enough to campaign for my point of view.

"I don't know how you can bear it," I sympathized. "I can see it's wearing you out, Honey."

He sighed. "Well, it seems to be making an old man of me. There's sure no future in wading around, neck-deep, in snow. Sometimes I don't think I can move through the stuff fast enough to even get out of the way of the falling trees."

"You mean you're thinking of going back to the bank?" I blurted eagerly.

His face fell. I knew immediately I'd pushed too hard.

"You just don't understand that I'm not made for an office, do you?" His voice was quiet, but I could hear the hurt in it.

Silence fell, like a curtain, between us.

"Something else will open up in the spring," he said at last, shoving back his chair.

I wanted to reach out for him. But I didn't. I felt torn in two! The demanding, "get ahead," frightened, part of me was warring with the part that wanted to be trusting and optimistic and hopeful. Why couldn't I concentrate on living each day fully, instead of on how much money the day had grossed?

It was thirty degrees below zero when John arrived home the next afternoon. By this time the timber he had been cutting had run out and he was cutting in Lincoln, sixty-five miles north of Helena. The new job was in a patch of lodgepole, a pine that grows surprisingly tall, considering its small diameter. It grows straight, with very few limbs. John figured there was about a month of cutting in the new patch. At first John had been excited about cutting lodgepole, there being so few tedious limbs to lop off. But tonight I could see he was more exhausted than ever.

He slowly pulled off his wet outer clothing.

"You look so tired, Honey," I said, coming over to hug him hard around the middle. "How was Lincoln?"

"Okay."

"Get a lot of trees down?"

"Yeah."

"Snow deep?"

He sighed. "About midthigh, I s'pose."

I loved him. I loved his simplicity, his honest lack of need for the riffraff of material goods. When I'd had a quiet day to think it over, I realized John's way of thinking was right. Maybe I could feel the way he did, too, if so many of my friends didn't have beautiful homes and other expensive possessions—if I didn't know they were "getting ahead" and I wasn't.

But I couldn't escape their world except for brief moments on some mountainside. How could I break away from my own desires and dreams?

John's silence screamed at me. I steeled myself for whatever he had to say when he warmed up enough to talk. I wanted to hear what was going on in his mind, but at the same time I was afraid to hear it.

"What's worrying you?" I urged him in a moment, keeping my hands busy setting the table.

"Oh, it's just a bad stretch of timber I'm into," he answered.

"What's the matter with it?" I prodded.

He turned his back to the fire. "Well, you know, how in most cuts the trees generally want to fall in one direction? Well, this lodgepole is too small to really wedge and they tend to go in all directions. They keep falling wrong and hitting other trees and hanging up."

I handed John his cup of hot chocolate. As he sipped it, he hooked a thumb through one suspender.

"I had a small tree hang up on another standing tree this afternoon," he continued quietly, "so I cut a second tree—a big one, about fifteen inches at the stump—and aimed it so it would hit the 'leaner' and knock it down."

Cradling his cup in both hands, John blew on the hot chocolate forcing the hot steam to tumble over the edge of the cup. He took a slow sip.

"It didn't knock the leaner down," he explained. "The leaner was wedged in the crook of that other tree. My hit tree was too tall; when it hit the leaner the butt jumped about fifteen feet in the air and kinda balanced there a minute like a teeter–totter. When the butt end came back down to the ground it was sliding my way.

"I was running out of the way but I knew I was in trouble. I tried to heave my saw off to the side so I could run faster, but when I did that, I tripped in the snow.

"I landed on my side and looked up to see that tree butt about ten feet away coming right at me. I knew I had to move—and fast. But I just couldn't get going in all that snow."

John looked up and grinned at me. I was staring at him in horror, the plates in my hands forgotten.

"I guess I just kinda braced myself," he went on, moving a little away from the fire.

"But God really took care of me, Peggy. That old tree stopped right at my boot."

I set down the plates and sank into a chair across the table from him. I swallowed hard.

"Well, there's more." John continued before I could comment. "I smashed my saw just before quitting time."

"Your chain saw?" I exclaimed involuntarily.

John kept talking as though he hadn't heard me. "Those tree tops are so thin and frozen so hard that if they hit another tree on the way down, the tops break off. I had just cut a tree down—it was laying on the ground—so I started my notch on another tree. All of a sudden, swoosh! A tree top came flying down, bounced off my hard hat and smashed into my saw. It cracked up the motor housing, but I don't think it hurt the motor. I figure maybe I can fiberglass the cover back together," he concluded, stretching, like a cat, in the comfortable warmth of the fire.

"Well, what about your head?" I asked anxiously.

"Oh, it feels okay," he retorted off-handedly.

Then he chuckled. "I guess I better show you my hard hat." John pulled himself out of his chair and shuffled, in stocking feet, out to the back porch.

He came back wearing the blue hard hat jauntily on his head. His eyes twinkled as he swept it off and handed it, upside down, to me.

I shook my head in disbelief. All the suspension straps were broken off the headband.

Suddenly we both were laughing. How wonderful it was to be safe—to know we were protected by angels!

Happily John was able to repair the motor casing so that it worked as well as before. Even our chain saw had been protected!

The next morning John called another logger he knew and was given a falling job in some bigger timber near Avon, west of Helena. Without any nagging on my part, he had quit that dangerous patch of lodgepole pine!

I was delighted. Perhaps John was changing, too.

Chapter 16

Over the Road and Sleeping Alone

"Spring break up"—when the mountain snows begin to melt and the roads turn into impassable mud slides—is vacation time for loggers. John bundled us all into our Subaru wagon to take us to Fairmont Hot Springs Resort, about one hundred miles from Helena.

The boys, and I, too, squealed with delight when we opened the door of our hotel room. What a luxury to be sleeping overnight in such a lovely room!

We played for hours in the warm swimming pool. When we tired of that, we soaked in the hot pool for a diversion. Later, Sammy and I napped in the quiet of our hotel room, while John and Justin and Joe played video games in the huge lobby of the resort. That evening, we dined in the hotel restaurant.

"Wow, Mom, isn't this neat?" Joey exclaimed as he gazed at the candlelit tables.

John reached over to squeeze my hand.

"It's good to relax a little, huh?" he smiled, the lines

around his eyes crinkling his weathered face.

"Oh it feels wonderful!" I breathed.

How good a day of rest could be! And how gratifying to see my boys' faces alight with their enjoyment of our rare holiday. I would carry the memory—and a new appreciation of John—with me. He had seen our need for a vacation and had provided it, when, at last, his schedule of hard work allowed it. I was more ashamed than ever that I had accused him of a lack of understanding.

Three days later John heard of a job for a fuel truck driver. With only one phone call, he landed the job.

"It's too good to be true!" John exclaimed. "I've dreamed of driving a tanker truck like this since the first time I got behind a steering wheel!"

I threw my arms around his neck. Truckers made good money, didn't they?

John drove the boys and me out to the truck terminal to see his rig.

"Can we go for a ride? Can we Daddy?" The boys ran ahead of us to the monstrous truck.

"Good heavens, John, it's a block long!" I exclaimed.

"Eighty-five feet from front bumper to the back of the pup," he corrected me.

"The pup?" I dubiously asked.

"Oh, that's the name for the little trailer on the back. You call the whole outfit a 'train' because there's three separate pieces—a tractor, a semi-trailer, and a pup."

"Lift me up, Dad! Can we get in?" the boys clamored.

"Well ... here, you can take a look. But no rides." John picked Joey up and held him in the crook of one arm while he pulled himself up the metal rungs to the door. I could see Joe's eyes widen as they reached the top.

"Gee, Dad, you mean you can push all those buttons?" Joe asked.

John climbed nimbly back down to help Justin up to the cab.

"Hey, who sleeps here?" Justin demanded.

"Oh, you call that a 'sleeper,' " John explained. "It's for the driver to sleep in if he gets tired. Here, you boys climb up in there and make room for your mother."

I mounted the last rung and looked around, awestruck myself.

"Gee, John, this is a pretty plush office!"

He laughed.

"No, I'm serious," I insisted. The seat was like a padded swivel desk chair. A panel of instruments wrapped around the steering wheel so that seemingly hundreds of switches and dials were at the driver's finger tips. A wide, leather-like console separated the driver and passenger side like a polished office desk.

"You call this the 'bench,' " John told me, thumping on the broad expanse of the console. "The engine is under it."

"And the sleeper—why it's as big as a double bed, wouldn't you say?" I asked.

"Oh these truckers like a comfortable cab," he beamed a trifle smugly.

"Hey," Justin shouted. "Is that a CB? Can I hold the microphone, Dad?"

"Sure." John unhooked the "mike" and handed it to him.

"Breaker one-nine! Any smokies out there? You got a copy? Over and out." Justin called.

John and I stared at each other.

"Trucker lingo?" I guessed.

"Yeah!" John nodded. He took a deep breath that seemed to puff out his chest. He was smiling broadly.

It wasn't long before my initial ecstasy was marred by the harsh reality of a trucker's lifestyle. John's hours were impossible. He worked a twelve-to-fourteen hour shift for about six nights in a row, then usually had a night off before he started the next six nights of work. Because we could never plan ahead which night he would get off, life soon seemed to stretch out in one long, monotonous routine. We could have no leisure time, either, as a couple or as a family, because John, always working by late afternoon, came in during the wee morning hours to sleep most of the day.

Still, with all of its drawbacks, I was delighted with the benefits of this trucking job. The steady paycheck and insurance policies and retirement program were the mainstay I'd been praying for. I fervently hoped John would stay happy, driving trucks until he was old enough for retirement.

That desire spurred me to tackle enthusiastically the solo parenting of the boys during John's long absences. I filled in the hours without John by joining a new women's Bible study group and getting away frequently for tea with a friend.

It was hard to keep the boys quiet while John slept through their playing hours; and, at night, I was afraid. After I had tucked the boys into bed and lingered to study their angel faces, the house seemed eerily quiet. It wasn't the boys I was worried about; I'd defend them like a mad lioness if anyone dared lay a hand on them.

No, I was frightened for myself—a woman alone. In my parents' home, at the college dorm, then married to John —I had never before spent nights alone. Every gruesome crime I had ever heard or read about attacked my nighttime imagination.

I tried to reason with myself: Our neighbors slept within screaming distance. The doors were securely locked. No matter; I would wake to the sound of imaginary footsteps in the house and cower, not daring to breathe or turn my head, waiting for a dim figure to appear in my bedroom doorway.

One evening, after tucking the boys into bed, I slipped outside to pray. It was a warm evening with a soft breeze of spring rustling the lilac trees. Their sweet scent caressed me like a kiss from my fatherly Creator.

As I prayed in that gentle darkness, my eyes were drawn to the white picket fence that skirted our yard. Suddenly each of those pickets were like soldiers guarding my home. I knew I was sensing the heavenly guardians, those angels more numerous than pickets on my fence, who were encamped about my house, protecting me.

"He will cover you with his feathers, and under his wings you will find refuge; his faithfulness will be your shield and rampart. You will not fear the terror of the night, nor the arrow that flies by day" (Ps. 91:4-5).

Dear old Psalm 91 sustained me again.

Later that night, when I undressed for bed and turned out the light, fear gripped me.

"I can't see!" I thought. "What is lurking in my house that I can't see?"

But Psalm 91, also, was firmly entrenched in my mind.

This time, instead of pushing my frightening thoughts away, I spoke softly, but firmly, to them.

"You are good, Thoughts," I told them. "You have blessed me with the ability to imagine angel guardians around my house tonight. But quiet down now and go to sleep," I directed them.

I snapped my bedside light on again and read aloud a comforting little verse:

"I will lie down and sleep in peace, for you alone, O LORD, make me dwell in safety" (Ps. 4:8).

I repeated the verse several times.

"You alone, O LORD, make me dwell in safety."

I remembered the angels, more numerous than pickets on my fence.

In a few moments I turned out the light and fell asleep the moment I closed my eyes.

Even I could see my old cowardly self changing, and in a way that could only be credited to the super power of God. Like Paul, I found I was not myself—I was living a life that was not my own, but a life of faith in Jesus who lived in me (Gal. 2:20).

Of course my figment prowlers weren't the only frightening sleep determent. I worried about the slippery roads on the mountain passes near Helena which John had to maneuver in a twenty-eight-wheel-tractor trailer-rig, loaded with flammable fuel.

On one of his first runs, an early May morning, a light rain had been falling, freezing when it hit the pavement. John was easing down the homeward slope of the Boulder Pass, sipping a hot cup of coffee.

He had flipped on his engine brake at the top of the hill. His two trailers were full, bringing his gross truck weight up to 110,000 pounds. With that much weight, John didn't want the truck to gain momentum he couldn't control on the slick roads.

Suddenly something steel gray flashed into his vision in the left-hand mirror. The trailers of his train were sliding sideways on the icy roadway! The back end of the semitrailer was in the left lane at about a forty-five-degree angle to the tractor. The pup was hidden from his view.

In one fluid movement, John splashed his coffee out the open window and touched the pup brakes lightly. At the same time, he accelerated slightly, which sent power to the drive wheels. The rig pulled smoothly back into line.

"It all happened so effortlessly—I didn't even get burned by the coffee!" John exclaimed later. "It was as if a guardian angel took over driving for me!"

John's usual run was a narrow twisted road that followed the Boulder River through its canyon toward Butte, Montana. On Friday and Saturday nights he was always cautious driving that road from ten o'clock till two. The traffic was usually heavier than on week nights; the drivers tended to speed up and take more chances. John referred to them as the "bar traffic."

One Saturday night a little after midnight, John was driving in a freezing spring rainstorm. The sanding crews were not yet out and the steep, winding road soon became covered with "black" ice. The wet black pavement seemed to swallow the light from the truck's powerful headlights rather than reflecting the beams on down the road.

A hundred yards after rounding a corner, John suddenly caught sight of a dark object ahead of him. He hit the brakes, locking up the wheels on his rig. The fuel-laden truck went into a slide, heading straight for an old Willy's Jeep blocking John's lane.

Headlights flashed into his line of vision as a car rounded a corner, five-hundred yards ahead. His options were dwindling. Should he hit the ditch?

Before the question really registered, John had made his choice: He threw on his warning flashers and released the truck brakes long enough to swerve his tractor and both trailers into the path of the oncoming car. He could only pray that the other driver would start braking immediately. If the other car couldn't stop, John knew he would have to run his truck over the left road bank into a creek bottom.

Pumping the brakes on and off, John was able to skid the rig to a stop alongside the stalled jeep. The oncoming car slid to a stop a few yards from John's front bumper.

John leaped out of the cab, running and sliding over to the jeep. A young man in his mid-twenties lay on the seat. As John opened the door, a beer can tumbled out, clattering onto the icy roadway.

John shook the unconscious young man. No response.

John pulled him upright and hollered, "Hey, guy! Wake up!"

The young man started, mumbled a few slurred syllables, and slumped back down on the seat.

By this time the other driver had crept across the road to the jeep. He looked as if he were a salesman: middle-aged, wearing a suit and tie under a heavy overcoat.

"He's drunk!" John shouted. "I'll shove this guy over and get this jeep off to the side of the road before someone gets killed!''

Grunting under the man's weight, John heaved the limp body against the passenger door. He swung back into the driver's seat, rattling empty beer cans with his boot as he felt for the clutch.

He turned the key. Nothing.

The salesman, who had been peering in through the open door, quickly suggested they push it to the side of the road.

"Let's try," John agreed.

He slammed the gearshift into neutral and jumped out of the jeep.

The salesman pushed on the front fender. John leaned his weight against the door frame, ready to turn the wheel with one hand when the vehicle began moving. But the road was so slick that the men couldn't get enough footing to push the jeep.

"Oh no! Something's coming!" the salesman cried as two headlights came barreling around the corner. "He'd better start slowing down or we're in big trouble!"

"It's a jeep!" John exclaimed as the vehicle weaved to a sliding stop behind them. "I'll see if he'll pull this dead one off the road." John skated back to the driver's open window.

"Hi!" he greeted the man unceremoniously, "Can you give us a pull . . . " he bit off the sentence. Inside the jeep was a deputy sheriff.

"Boy am I glad to see you!" John whooped.

After making hurried explanations to the deputy, John turned back to his truck.

"If you fellas don't mind, I'm gonna get out of here before somebody comes flying around that corner and hits my load of fuel!" he called over his shoulder.

"I'll get out of your way," volunteered the salesman, creeping unsteadily toward his car.

As John reached up to open the door on his cab, he was hit by a blast of hot air. He had left his coat in the cab when he jumped out of the truck—for the first time he realized he was shivering and soaking wet.

The salesman's tires spun as he backed out of John's way.

John shifted his truck into gear. The tandem drive wheels spun helplessly on the ice. In a few seconds, however, the drivers melted through the ice and the truck began to inch forward, melting more ice as it went.

After burning off about ten feet of ice, John backed up his rig. Shifting into low gear, he was able to get enough momentum on the ten feet of bare pavement to keep the truck moving onto the icy roadway and on to Butte.

John was secretly beginning to wonder why he had once thought truck driving so glamorous. Chronic tiredness plagued him. Fears of falling asleep behind the wheel haunted him.

"This is such a pretty drive," I remarked to him one summer day a few years later as we wound through the pine trees along the narrow Boulder River road.

"It is," John agreed. "But I remember times when I hated it, especially on summer Sunday mornings like this. The sun would be coming up behind that same mountain, making shadows through the trees across the pavement, only, on those mornings I'd be the only one on the road. I knew everyone else was home on Sunday morning while I had been driving all night. All I wanted at times like that was to be a normal husband and father, sleeping and waking up when my family did."

Despite John's growing weariness he stayed with his steady trucking job. I was no longer afraid when he drove. Hadn't God proven time and again that John was safe in the shadow of His wings?

"He will call upon me, and I will answer him; I will be with him in trouble, I will deliver him and honor him. With long life I will satisfy him and will show him my salvation" (Ps. 91:15–16).

Then one night during the independent trucker's strike John called me from the phone booth at the truck terminal at midnight.

"Sorry to wake you up," he apologized. "But I wanted you to be praying for me. There's a report that truckers have been shot at in Great Falls and Bozeman and even East Helena."

John had already heard of reports of violence on the road. From overpasses, independents had dangled plastic garbage bags full of oil so they would be hit by the windshields of passing semi-trucks. Nighttime drivers couldn't see the suspended bag until it was too late.

There were also reports of huge boulders being dropped from overpasses to smash through the windshields of trucks passing underneath.

John was already wary of overpasses. In the early summer he had hauled a load of jet fuel from Salt Lake City to Helena. It was about 11 p.m. when he pulled through Idaho Falls on Interstate Highway 15. As he approached an overpass, he noticed a group of dark figures leaning over the side.

"Kids out watching the traffic," he guessed. Suddenly John saw something falling. He wrenched the wheel hard to the left, but not in time. With a dull thud, a water balloon hit the passenger side of the windshield.

Because of the reported violence caused by the strike, John had begun switching on his fog lights when he neared an overpass at night. With the assistance of those two powerful spotlights, John peered through the darkness to detect any movement on the road above. Just before going under he would jerk his truck into the left lane.

The icy hand of fear gripped me as I hung up the phone after John's midnight call. My heart was pounding. What if something happened to John? I must stay awake and pray.

"Call Betty!" a voice seemed to whisper.

Without taking time to consider how late at night I was calling, I dialed Betty and Ted's number.

She answered sleepily.

"Oh, Betty," I apologized. "I'm so sorry to wake you. But it's John . . . "

"What is it? What's happened?" she was immediately wide awake.

I told her all about the strike and the shooting incidents.

"Why, we'll just pray Psalm 91 together," Betty told me. "Have you ever read it? I pray it whenever I'm worried."

As Betty read those beautiful old words to me, the cold grip of fear loosened its hold.

"A thousand may fall at your side, ten thousand at your right hand, but it will not come near you" (v.7).

I hung up the phone and lay back down on my pillow. How peaceful I felt! God was my trust.

That night as John was pulling the Boulder hill, he thought he saw something strange on the road ahead. But like a mirage, it seemed to disappear as he came closer.

"That's funny," he said to himself. "Am I so spooked I'm imagining things?"

John drove about a quarter of a mile farther when suddenly he thought he noticed something on the road again. Suspicious, he turned on his fog lights, but he had already driven over whatever it was.

Less than a half mile farther it appeared again. John strained to see. A roundish pool of something lay in his lane.

John's eyes widened. Roofing nails! Their gray color had blended with the pavement.

John swerved to the left, but his right-hand steering and driver tires ran over the nails.

He stopped at the top of the hill to check his tires. But he did not find a single nail!

The Sheriff's Department later confirmed the hill had been laced with two-inch roofing nails—thirty-two pounds of them. They were big-headed nails—the kind that would have flipped up when driven over. If they missed the lead tires they should have punctured the rear tires. It seemed impossible that all twenty-eight tires had gone over the nails without harm—impossible, but true.

Chapter 17

I Gotta Be Me

By late August I was enjoying the life of a trucker's wife. My fears for myself alone at night and for John on the road had dissolved. When they did come knocking at my mind, they were easily dismissed with a quick prayer: "I trust you, Lord, I know You are faithful to what You promise in Psalm 91." And I did know. He had saved us from danger so many times, how could I doubt He would go on watching over us?

"There is really only one drawback to John's trucking job," I admitted to my friend Melissa one afternoon in late August. "I'm just so out of patience with the boys."

"It must be hard to have John gone all the time," Melissa comforted me. "You need the break of having him come home and take the boys off your hands for awhile."

Melissa had been a close friend since college days. She was unpretentious and always put me at ease. I could trust her to accept me no matter what I confided.

"Sometimes I just wish I could sort of recharge my mother-batteries," I told her. "Think what single parents go through!"

"Yep!" Melissa agreed. I could hear the dishes clattering in her sink as we talked on the phone. "It's probably a good thing they usually end up working to support their kids. They'd go crazy being home all the time, especially with no husband to walk in the door and at least carry on a conversation with them."

Justin slammed the kitchen door. I turned around to glance at him just in time to see his fingers leave four streaks of black across the kitchen door. He left another trail of mud on the floor.

"Oh no," I muttered into the phone. "Mud pie time again!" It was too late now. I could already hear the bathroom water faucets running. Sink, floor, door knobs, and towels would all bear the stamp of the mud man by now.

I sighed and turned back to scour my frying pan. The telephone receiver was cradled between my ear and my right shoulder.

"Have you talked to John about trying to get the dispatchers to set up some kind of reasonable schedule?" Melissa was asking.

"No. He really can't," I said. "He just has to be on call to take runs whenever they need him. At least until he uses up all the hours in his log book."

Joey streaked into the kitchen holding a toy truck high over his head. Sam toddled after him, his chubby arms stretched out for the truck.

Sam had begun walking at fifteen months. Although his eyes still did not appear to hold a focus, he seemed to see everything. He trotted fearlessly through the house, dodging furniture as adroitly as any toddler.

Melissa's voice jolted my attention back to the telephone conversation. "Peggy, you're so thoughtful not to nag John about his long hours."

"Thoughtful?" I laughed. "It's really rather selfish. I don't say anything because I don't want to lose his nice paycheck. I've got to go now, Melis," I finished quickly, as Joey and Sam both screeched, pulling on opposite ends of the truck. I slammed the telephone receiver into its cradle and scampered across the floor, retrieving the truck just as Sam lost his hold and crashed down on his diapered behind.

"Waaaaaaa!" They both screamed at once.

"Come on," I ordered them, picking Sam up and propelling Joe ahead of me to the boys' bedroom. "Let's see if we can find you each another toy."

But my mind was still on my conversation with Melissa. Surely if I was independent enough to sleep without John in the house at night, I was independent enough to find my own child-care solution, I told myself.

Melissa's comment about a single parent needing to get out of the house made sense. It would be better for the children, too, if their mother spent a little time away from home so that she could come back refreshed.

Why not ask my neighbor Mary to watch the boys one day a week? She baby-sat children in her home every day. I could spend that one day a week doing whatever I wished. What a luxury! And what a panacea for the cabin fever doldrums—looking forward to one special day each week that was mine.

Mary agreed to take the boys on Wednesdays.

The first thing on my "special morning" agenda was: attend mass. How much easier it was to concentrate on

the prayers and Scriptures without children on my lap!
Often I went shopping, had lunch with a friend, and
spent the afternoon in the quiet of the library. I didn't
need to do anything exotic or expensive; merely having
time to myself, without small distractions, proved therapeutic.

The best idea that sprang from my Wednesday adventures was trying my hand at writing. I wrote of my frustrations. I wrote of my joys. I felt better. My feelings
became manageable when they could come merrily slipping and sliding out of me into the light of day.

After about a month, Bonnie told me of a Christian
writers fellowship in Helena. I attended the monthly
meetings and discovered that Elaine Wright Colvin, the
founder of the club, had the know-how I needed to market some of my stories. It was the modest beginning of a
fulfilling part-time career.

My self-image soared. Why hadn't I realized sooner
the importance of making time for myself, setting some
goals, and seeking after them?

Making a decision to do something about my problems was one of the best moves I ever made. It cleared
my head. I realized now that I could change things myself—with a little prayer and ingenuity. It was time for
me to meet my attitude of silently blaming John—when
our money supply was low or when I missed the security
of the bank job—head on. He had always provided
enough for our needs; if I needed more money in order
to feel secure I should take charge of finding it myself.

I could get a job of my own. Just one glance at such an
alternative was enough for me, however; I loved the freedom of being a stay-at-home wife. (Maybe John and I

were more alike than I thought.) Knowing that, if I really wanted, I could do something about my financial situation silenced my complaining spirit.

John was glad I was finding new interests.

"You wrote that?" he exclaimed when I mustered up all my bravado and showed him the first of my writings. "Hey, I'm really impressed!"

"You know, you make me so proud of you," he told me one morning when he arrived home for a midmorning meal. "I just admire anyone who can ... well ... say things on paper, you know?"

I did know. He was loving something in me the way I loved and admired things in him. Like his courage or his ingenuity to invent little gadgets that made his motors tick. I could never be provoked with him for long when I remembered what an amazing man he was.

Feeling that I was special—that I had unique and admirable talents—made me all the more grateful to God. And it gave me a freedom to feel good about myself. That feeling benefited my whole family.

I was no longer frustrated by the boys' constant interruptions because I was allowing time for myself. I was no longer holding up a wall of resentment between John and me; I was free of some imagined martyrdom. I was not a victim of circumstances.

One other thing that needed changing was my competitive desire for "things"—such as a new house. God combined many lessons in order to teach me to love my old house, but probably the most dramatic lesson was taught me by Lavinia, a woman who leaned over my fence one summer morning.

"Looks like you could put some old rusty nails down

in the soil around that apple tree," she informed me. "Needs iron."

I set down my laundry basket and strolled over to the fence, eyeing my apple tree with new interest. Maybe old nails *were* what it needed. The tree was like me—in need of so many ingredients to make it perfect and whole.

Lavinia's thick hair shone bluish black in the sun. Her cocoa brown eyes seemed to take in everything; her flawless olive skin shone like satin in the warm sunlight. She seemed akin to the out-of-doors in a way that I— with sunburned cheeks and peeling nose—could only envy.

Lavinia was recently divorced. She had left her alcoholic husband in California and, with her three sons, had headed north in a twelve-foot camper trailer. She had found a job painting fences and doing other odd jobs at a nearby Helena ranch.

Lavinia's ancestors were French Canadian, she told me later. Her mother had emigrated and married a black college professor. Lavinia's husband had been a college professor, too; and she, a suburban California housewife. I wondered which intriguing parts of her lineage had blessed her with the strength and courage to live as she was when I met her.

Lavinia and her three children ate a meal with us. A few days later I drove out to her camper trailer. I brought along a few things her boys obviously lacked.

"Come in! Come in!" Lavinia welcomed me, stepping out of the camper as I parked my car and opened the door. The trailer rested under a shade tree. Perhaps it protected her home from the sun most of the day; but now, around supper time, the sun's merciless rays had slipped around to beat through its postage stamp windows.

"Here, boys," she called to her curly-headed children. "We're having their favorite—pork 'n' beans and jumbo hot dogs," she explained to me. The bigger boys were about sixteen and thirteen years of age. The oldest one carried the youngest, a two-year-old, over to the campground picnic table.

"May I help?" I offered.

"Oh, no, they'll help themselves," Lavinia declined, stooping to retrieve a sleeping bag and pile of clothes from the narrow walkway in the camper. The place was almost wall-to-wall mattresses and hammocks. I couldn't guess where she stored cooking utensils or the family clothing. A tiny sink and miniature stove stood as her only meager conveniences.

I followed Lavinia back outside as she toted hot dog buns and paper plates. The boys wolfed the food down.

I shrank back from the wooden picnic table; in a tree, overhead, a swarm of hornets buzzed around their nest. An angry welt was already budding on the baby's forehead.

How can she endure it? I wondered, watching Lavinia directing the boys' supper. How could anyone live in a little camper too small to accommodate a table, too stifling hot to warrant closing the door to keep out a swarm of hornets? I couldn't bear the thought of my boys living like this—I would lose my mind!

Within a few days Lavinia was gone, headed south to Arizona to find work. But Lavinia's lesson sank deeply into my mind. It touched off a new attitude of gratitude for my old house.

How wonderful to raise a family of boys in such spaciousness! Our large yard boasted its tall old shade trees; Lavinia's trailer nearly fit inside each of my high-ceilinged rooms. Why had I wanted a modern house with cramped living areas and an unimaginative, box-like design?

I found myself falling in love, all over again, with the character and roominess of our home. And there was so much more fixing I could do. I had wallpapered and painted the rooms warm yellow and peach, accented with browns and oranges. Bonnie, my generous neighbor, helped me recover our sturdy old couch and taught me to macramé a pretty floor-to-ceiling plant hanger. I sewed new curtains and throw pillows, I found second-hand furniture which I restored to its former beauty. At garage sales I bought wicker baskets, pretty old vases, and candlesticks. With a little scrubbing and painting they looked like new. On a stroll through a mountain pasture, I found dried flowers, which I arranged for my living room.

Again I thanked Lavinia for opening my eyes. How foolish to have thought I would have been happy doling out the large payments on a new house every month. There were so many possibilities for remodeling what we had—the basement to finish, the second story to expand. Everything we needed stood within these four walls. What more could I have wanted?

Gently and mysteriously God was removing my persistent desires for so many material things. He was filling the emptiness of disappointment with joy in what I had.

This transformation was not unlike the change in me after I saw the dream of how we were chosen as Sam's parents. One quieting glance at the alternatives that life had offered a less fortunate woman than I, and I hurried back to the happy security of things as they were.

Chapter 18

The Trail Bends Again

I was at the kitchen counter mixing bread dough when John first mentioned rabbits.

"Rabbit meat is selling for over two dollars a pound out on the coast," he informed me as he reached for the phone.

"Hmm?" I encouraged him. Was this the sixth cup of flour or was I up to number seven?

"Amazingly, the only butcher in the state is right out of ... Hello? Yes, I'm calling to get the price of a ton of rabbit pellets," John continued.

The yeast! No wonder the stuff felt so dry. I forgot the yeast!

I dumped the yeast and water mixture over the dough and started kneading the slimy ball with my hands. Yuck, what a mess!

"Bless this poor old bread, Lord," I muttered.

John hung up the telephone and sat down at the kitchen table. He contemplated his list of figures on vitamins, soy content, and rabbit medication, which he had scribbled on the back of this month's Montana Power bill.

"Go on, Honey," I urged over my shoulder, "Tell me about rabbits."

"Oh yeah, well, these rabbits are very prolific. You raise them on a confined, indoor operation and they have a new batch of young every month. Now, it just happens that the only butcher in the state is out by Canyon Ferry, twenty miles out of Helena. This butcher will buy all the bunnies we can raise. He has contracts with refrigerated trucks that haul the meat out to the coast."

Sam had wedged himself between the cupboard and me and was pushing on my knees, forcing me to back up about two feet away from the cupboard, while still keeping my hands in the bread dough.

"Wa–wa!" he stated emphatically.

I rubbed off as much of the sticky bread dough as I could and sidestepped around Sam to the sink.

"Here, Honey," I told him holding the cup of water gingerly in my fingers.

"Rabbit meat. Who would buy it?" I wondered.

John's voice rambled around me as I gazed out the kitchen window to the snowy yard and street.

John had quit his truck driving job in the fall. He told me he could no longer justify spending so much time away from home. Besides, the long night hauls left him exhausted.

Sometimes John had grown so drowsy he had pulled his rig over to the shoulder of the road and stopped. There he'd fall asleep with his head on the steering wheel. After a few minutes John would jerk awake. Terrified, he would stomp the brake pedal, thinking he had fallen asleep at the wheel while the truck was still moving.

In the mountains north of Helena, John found a job chipping slate rock, used for fireplaces and decorative rock walls. John and his partner Geno worked together in the raw winter winds that swept down the mountain sides. There was no shelter except for scattered Ponderosa pines and sagebrush jutting up here and there through the crusty snow. The wages were small, but enough. The eight hour daytime shift relaxed all of us.

In many ways this winter had been kind to John and me. I was finding a new fulfillment and self-confidence in writing articles and sending them off to magazines. John had found new self-confidence, too. He had proven he could support his family outside the office setting. So far the "right" job hadn't come his way, but he knew it would, he just kept doggedly searching.

A few days after our kitchen conversation, John drove to the northern part of the state to observe some rabbitries. He accumulated all kinds of data from the helpful people he met, from letters to agricultural bureaus, and from library books.

John's shorter hours made us feel more rested; we were both ready to dream again about that "perfect" job. This rabbit farm could be it! If we sold our house, we figured, we could make a down payment on a small piece of land in the country. We could live in a trailer house and build a first-class, heated barn for our three-hundred doe rabbits. I knew there would be moments when I would regret leaving my beloved old house—for a trailer. But if we could find one of reasonable size— say, fourteen by seventy—I could always console myself on bad days by remembering Lavinia's twelve-footer.

In late December, even though John was still unsatisfied with the figures he had collected on rabbit feed consumption, we put our house on the market. We would leave it up to the Lord: If our house sold, we would know He wanted us to move to the country and raise rabbits; if it didn't sell, we would have no money to invest in our dreams.

In spite of my reservations about living in a cramped trailer house and both John's and my aversion to going deeply into debt, I was excited about our future. Country living sounded ideal for our three boys, and having John working at something that would not take him away from home seemed the answer to our prayers. In fact, the rabbit business seemed so perfect that we were sure the Lord had been leading us here all along.

One Monday morning I called the newspaper office to place an ad to sell our house. As I hung up the phone, sheer panic washed over me. I remembered feeling this terror when our first workhorse had tried to jump out of the truck. Was this feeling some kind of premonition?

The fear soon passed, however, and to our amazement, the first people who looked at the house bought it for thirty-two thousand dollars!

We had two months to find the land and a trailer house. Just as before, we quickly discovered the difficulty of finding a piece of ground not protected by covenants that banned commercial operations. But, after two weeks of searching, we found the perfect twenty acres of farm land.

Finding a used mobile home seemed harder. Trailers large enough for our family cost more than we had anticipated. Twice we made offers on trailer houses that we thought would accommodate us, but each offer was refused.

One day our realtor called. We could not buy the farm land we had picked out; the owner had changed his mind about selling.

"Why is it so hard to find the right place, Lord?" we pleaded. But no answer came.

We did make one purchase: an old '58 Ford septic pumping truck, at a bargain price. With it, John would pump out the refuse in his rabbits' waste pit.

Early in January our rabbit dream fell apart. With only two weeks remaining before our house sale would close, we had no trailer house and no land.

John came home early that afternoon and planted himself grimly in front of the kitchen fire.

"What's wrong?" I demanded, a cold feeling knifing through my stomach.

He turned and stared hard at me. "You remember that big rabbitry—the one all the others in Montana base their operating costs on?"

I nodded slowly.

"Well, they're out of business—bankrupt. I knew something was wrong with their feed costs! And the price of grain is going to go up," he added bitterly. "Some people are predicting it will triple. We'll go broke raising rabbits," he concluded looking up at me guiltily.

"Well, better to find out now than after we'd built the barn," I pointed out lamely.

Both John and I were frightened. Where would we go when our house sale closed? Having our rabbit dream punctured was bad enough. But losing the security and shelter of our old house? What was the Lord trying to tell us?

But the worst news hit the next day when a man from the bank called. Our old house had appraised for forty-two thousand dollars. We had sold it for ten thousand dollars less than its worth!

The old greed for "more" reared its head. How *dare* God let us throw ten thousand dollars away, when we were already short of funds? Ten thousand dollars!

"We just keep praying and looking at Jesus," John reminded me, his old strength returning in this new crisis. "Remember Romans 8:28, Peggy: 'We know that in all things God works for the good of those who love him.' He knows our situation. He has a plan."

"Lord," John prayed aloud before we crawled into bed that night, "we have placed our lives into Your hands. That is where they will stay."

"Well," I sighed, "I know you're right." Then I wailed, "Oh John, I want to trust Him. I just wish I could be sure He and I saw eye to eye on what standard of living is best for me!"

John laughed and hugged me close. As always, just feeling John's arms around me eased my burden.

A few days later, the banker phoned again.

"Mrs. Brooke," he began, "we have a little problem with your property. But I'm sure you can iron everything out for us. Our surveyor tells me that six inches of your garage is sitting on your neighbor's property. Now, I'm sure your neighbor would give you an easement, but until this is cleared up, we can't loan the buyer his mortgage money."

Could it be? I hardly dared breathe as I hung up the

phone. Yes, it must be so! The Lord had provided us with a last minute "out" on selling our house.

We exercised our option of not obtaining an easement for our garage, and our old house was ours to keep.

I was so relieved and thankful for not being "on the street" that I wasn't even disappointed any more that our rabbit-raising idea had died. Besides, my ever-ingenious husband was already working on a new plan.

We might as well put the pumper truck we'd purchased to work, he figured. The truck, together with John's plumbing and "fix-it" talent, ought to work well together. We ordered a business phone and placed an ad in the Yellow Pages, listing our septic tank pumping business.

I felt secure and warm with the assurance that our old roof and walls would stay wrapped around me. John was happy, too, puttering away his spare time, getting the old pumper truck in working order for the day in mid-May when our first advertisement would appear.

During those first days of waiting for the telephone to ring and bring us some business, John came across a Scripture that we prayed often—and still pray today when bills pile up and our income is down.

"Though the fig tree does not bud
   and there are no grapes on the vines,
though the olive crop fails
   and the fields produce no food,
though there are no sheep in the pen
   and no cattle in the stalls,
yet will I rejoice in the LORD,
   I will be joyful in God my Savior"

(Hab. 3:17–18).

The Scripture summed up so much of what God had been teaching John and me over and over. And, although we often jokingly referred to God's path for us as "the scenic route" (He seemed to lead us on the most crooked way rather than on a straight path), we could now see He always had His reasons.

Even in times when my love for John stretched a little thin, in the end, the stretch marks made our love stronger. "And the two shall become one flesh" (Matt. 19:5). Over the years that was what had been happening to us, all right. It seemed that, in those hardest times when my selfishness and frustrations came to the surface and John saw me at my worst—and when I came to know his weaknesses as well—our love was made solid. Our oneness became real. No matter what, we needed each other. And God.

I was so grateful that God had given such a man to the thoughtless young girl I was when John married me. I was more in love with him than ever—and it wasn't John who had done all the changing!

Our new business prospered. Soon we had a new truck and expanded our services. More important, John was his own boss, just as he had always hoped. His work was out-of-doors and free from the restrictions of an office. Of course, since nothing is ever wasted in God's plan, John's accounting background paid off when it came to the hair-tearing business of keeping the books.

"You know," John said one night as he turned out the light, "sometimes it seems like we've been climbing a mighty tall mountain since I left the bank. And now, in a way, we've finally gotten to the top. Do you ever think that?"

If he had planned on falling right to sleep, he should have postponed that question.

"Oh, I don't know, Honey," I answered, smiling in the darkness. "I think our climb started long before you left the bank. I can trace it back at least as far as the day we met. And as for mountains, I think maybe we've crossed a whole range of them. God introduced you to me just so He could get me out of my comfortable little shell."

"I suppose that's true," John reflected. "The part about being comfortable, anyway. You never would have had so many struggles if you hadn't married me."

"No," I replied, snuggling closer. "But I think it was all meant to . . . jar me loose from all the familiar things I trusted . . . to show me that God is the One I should have been trusting to guide me over any mountain."

"Well, I really think God's got us where He wants us now. I like to think we have kinda arrived. Don't you?"

I yawned. "There's something I've been meaning to tell you, John," I said as casually as I could. "I . . . I think I'm pregnant."

John bolted upright. He snapped on the light.

"Really?" he asked, his eyes shining.

"Really." I echoed, blinking my eyes in the light.

"Well that just goes to show you that the climb is never finished—this side of heaven, anyway," he chuckled. "I guess we've just rounded another corner of the trail!"

CHRISTIAN HERALD ASSOCIATION AND ITS MINISTRIES

CHRISTIAN HERALD ASSOCIATION, founded in 1878, publishes The Christian Herald Magazine, one of the leading interdenominational religious monthlies in America. Through its wide circulation, it brings inspiring articles and the latest news of religious developments to many families. From the magazine's pages came the initiative for CHRISTIAN HERALD CHILDREN'S HOME and THE BOWERY MISSION, two individually supported not-for-profit corporations.

CHRISTIAN HERALD CHILDREN'S HOME, established in 1894, is the name for a unique and dynamic ministry to disadvantaged children, offering hope and opportunities which would not otherwise be available for reasons of poverty and neglect. The goal is to develop each child's potential and to demonstrate Christian compassion and understanding to children in need.

Mont Lawn is a permanent camp located in Bushkill, Pennsylvania. It is the focal point of a ministry which provides a healthful "vacation with a purpose" to children who without it would be confined to the streets of the city. Up to 1000 children between the ages of 7 and 11 come to Mont Lawn each year.

Christian Herald Children's Home maintains year-round contact with children by means of an *In-City Youth Ministry*. Central to its philosophy is the belief that only through sustained relationships and demonstrated concern can individual lives be truly enriched. Special emphasis is on individual guidance, spiritual and family counseling and tutoring. This follow-up ministry to inner-city children culminates for many in financial assistance toward higher education and career counseling.

THE BOWERY MISSION, located at 227 Bowery, New York City, has since 1879 been reaching out to the lost men on the Bowery, offering them what could be their last chance to rebuild their lives. Every man is fed, clothed and ministered to. Countless numbers have entered the 90-day residential rehabilitation program at the Bowery Mission. A concentrated ministry of counseling, medical care, nutrition therapy, Bible study and Gospel services awakens a man to spiritual renewal within himself.

These ministries are supported solely by the voluntary contributions of individuals and by legacies and bequests. Contributions are tax deductible. Checks should be made out either to CHRISTIAN HERALD CHILDREN'S HOME or to THE BOWERY MISSION.

Administrative Office: 40 Overlook Drive, Chappaqua, New York 10514
Telephone: (914) 769-9000